Law of Attraction Lover

This Book Includes: Manifestation Secrets Demystified, Script to Manifest & The Love of Attraction

By Elena G. Rivers

Copyright Elena G. Rivers © 2020

All rights reserved. No part of this publication may be reproduced, stored in a retrieval system, or transmitted, in any form or by any means, electronic, mechanical, photocopying, recording, or otherwise, without the prior written permission of the author and the publishers.

The scanning, uploading, and distribution of this book via the Internet or via any other means without the permission of the author is illegal and punishable by law. Please purchase only authorized electronic editions and do not participate in or encourage electronic piracy of copyrighted materials.

Elena G. Rivers © Copyright 2020 - All rights reserved.

ISBN: 978-1-80095-063-4

Legal Notice:

This book is copyright protected. It for personal use only.

Disclaimer Notice:

Please note the information contained in this book is for inspirational and entertainment purposes only. Every attempt has been made to provide accurate, up to date, and completely reliable information. No warranties of any kind are expressed or implied. Readers acknowledge that the author is not engaging in the rendering of legal, financial, health, medical, or professional advice. By reading this book, the reader agrees that under no circumstances are we responsible for any losses, direct or indirect, which are incurred as a result of the use of the information contained within this book, including, but not limited to, errors, omissions, or inaccuracies.

The information provided in this book is for entertainment purposes only. If you are struggling with serious problems, including chronic illness, mental instability, or legal issues, please consult with your local registered health care or legal professional as soon as possible. This book is not a substitute for professional or legal advice.

Contents

Part 1 – Book 1 9

Manifestation Secrets Demystified 9

Advanced Law of Attraction Techniques to Manifest Your Dream Reality by Changing Your Self-Image Forever 9

From the Author – Your Personalized LOA Cookbook 11

The #1 The Most Powerful Manifestation Principle That Took Me Years to Learn (+ the 3 Magical Words That Can Instantly Change Your Reality!) 18

The Indisputable Law of Self-Image 26

Secret#1 The Number One Question You Absolutely Can't Ignore 32

Secret#2 Trying to Re-Program Your Subconscious Mind? Discover Why It Might NOT Work Unless You De-Program It First 39

Secret #3 The Missing Links between Desire and Aligned Action (and the Best Manifestation Shortcut) 57

Secret #4 Manifest Faster By Slowing Down! (The #1 Thing to Learn from Mindful Manifestors) 65

Secret#5 Does Your Environment Block Your Manifestations? (Feng Shui It Up to Show the Universe You are Ready to Receive!) 71

Part 2 – Book 2 79

Script to Manifest 79

It's Time to Design & Attract Your Dream Life (Even if You Think it's Impossible Now) 79

Script to Manifest Your Desires 81

The Life-Changing Secrets of Scripting Revealed 92

    Using Numbers to Manifest Faster 97

The 3x33 method and its variations for busy people 98

Do You Speak, Think, and Act to Manifest? Or Do You Block Your Manifestations Without Even Knowing? 100

How do you know how to make the right decision and script about the right things? 102

The Hidden Dangers of Not Letting Go 107

The Ivory Tower Scripting Trap to Avoid! 111

Chapter 2 118

LOA for Skeptics (Why It Will Work for You If You Choose So!) 118

Chapter 3 122

Why You Can't Afford Not to Protect Your Dreams! ... 122

The Secrets to True Empowerment with Scripting 125

Chapter 5 134

Your Questions Answered 134

Chapter 6 147

Powerful Law of Attraction Meditation to Connect with Your Higher Self 147

Part 3 – Book 3 153

The LOVE of Attraction 153

Tested Secrets to Let Go of Fear-Based Mindsets, Activate LOA Faster, and Start Manifesting Your Desires! 153

Why the LOVE of Attraction? 155

Why It's ALL About Mindfully Mastering the Basics .. 160

Pillar#1 Your Authentic Alignment 176

Pillar #2 Your Desire Must be Authentic and So Must Be Your Energy 177

Pillar#3 Process Negative Energy Fast 178

Pillar#4 Love vs. Fear-Based Mindset 180

Pillar 5# Know Your Authentic Frequency 183

Pillar#6 Release Wanting and Doubting 184

Pillar#7 When Focusing on "Why Not's" Can Be Good for You 186

Secret #1 Realize When Your Subconscious Mind Goes Against You and Change the Disk 188

Secret #2 Do You Choose to Feel Light or Heavy? 193

Secret #3 Choosing Your Vibration 196

Secret#4 The Power of the Why Behind the Why 201

Secret#5 Releasing Low Vibrations and Using Certainty for Your Highest Good 203

Secret #6 Not All Negative Programming Is Really Negative 208

Secret#7 Release This Invisible Manifestation Killer 216

Secret#8 The Liberating Essence of Letting Go 218

Secret#9 Your Healthy, Love-Based Boundaries 222

Secret #10 When Making Mistakes is Important If You Want to Attract Abundance 233

Personal Message from Elena 237

Free LOA Newsletter + Bonus Gift 238

More Books by Elena G. Rivers 241

Part 1 – Book 1

Manifestation Secrets Demystified

Advanced Law of Attraction Techniques to Manifest Your Dream Reality by Changing Your Self-Image Forever

Law of Attraction Short Reads, Book 6

By Elena G. Rivers

Copyright Elena G. Rivers © 2020

From the Author – Your Personalized LOA Cookbook

"Elena, I don't think you should write this book. It's too generic. You didn't niche down properly. What about designing your reader avatar? I mean, are you writing for men or women? Are your readers already successful with manifestation? Or are they new to it? On a scale from 1-10, how would you rate their success level using Law of Attraction Principles? Honestly, judging from your outline, I don't think you should waste your time writing this book. What if people get confused?".

These were the words of a friend of mine, a very successful digital marketer and sociologist. He just wanted to help me and shared his honest feedback. As a very logical person, all the decisions he takes are based on data and only data.

I certainly don't think he's a naysayer. In fact, he's a very positive person. But, when it comes to marketing, he's pretty set in his ways. And yes, he's very successful with what he does. Following his recipe for success serves him well.
However, there's also intuition and creativity. And this feeling inside your gut telling you to do something.

So, this is how I got the idea to write this book. Even though many people, suggested otherwise.

But, I still decided to write it despite my friend's words that I didn't have enough data to write it correctly.

What does "correct" mean anyway? And why am I starting this book in such a weird way?

It's simple - we are all different, and we all resonate with different things. We can't all think and act the same way, imagine we did, the world would be so dull!

Long-term happiness and abundance are created thanks to balance. It's all about balancing logic and data with intuition and creativity.

At the same time, two people may perceive the same thing differently. For example, my friend thinks that my reader avatar is not clearly defined in terms of demographics: "I mean, Elena, are you writing for men or women? And how old are they?"

At the same time, my heart tells me: *"You can go ahead and write this book Elena, you already know your reader avatar. You write for ambitious souls, that's it. And you also know you don't write for people who expect instant fixes or lottery wins without attempting to add any value to the world."*

So, here I am, writing a book with a slightly different structure than my other books in *the Law of Attraction Short Reads* series. While most of my other books are written as systems and programs with specific steps to follow, this book is more like a creative recipe book with no particular order to follow.

It's a creative recipe book for the mind to help you align with the right manifestation principle for you and your current journey. Take what you like and reject the rest.

Imagine you get a new cookbook with a ton of recipes in it. Even if such a cookbook is related to a diet you particularly enjoy, there's no way you'd like all the recipes it contains. You'd most likely pick a few you think will taste good. Then, you'd keep making them so that you can get better and better.

Would you even try to force yourself to make a recipe you know you won't enjoy, judging from the ingredient list or a preparation method?

Of course not.

Yet, when it comes to manifestation and the Law of Attraction, it seems like so many people desperately try to torture themselves with techniques and exercises they don't even resonate with.

For example, some people, such as myself, are scripting and journaling junkies. And so, it's no wonder that any manifestation methods that involve writing, for example, writing things you're grateful for, work well for them.

When you love what you do, you feel good and raise your vibration. It's as simple as that.

But some people don't like the idea of daily writing and journaling. Perhaps, they would do better with a different manifestation method or a slight variation of it. Perhaps, they can write something only once and stick it to their vision board. Or maybe they'd enjoy affirmations more than writing? Or perhaps daily visualization is what makes them tick?
So, be sure to choose a recipe you like. Don't force yourself into practicing LOA methods you don't enjoy, as that can create stress and resistance.

Stress and resistance lead to contraction and negativity. And to manifest beautiful things into your life, you need to focus on expansion and positivity.

The most important thing to focus on is who you are – your mindset and energy are everything.

Back to our cookbook example: a person can choose a fantastic recipe, but since they are not adequately focused and remain negative, they will make a few mistakes while cooking, therefore spoiling their efforts.

So, it's so important to feel positive and expectant while having fun with the process of "cooking your dream reality." Use this rule for any mental or spiritual exercise you choose to do.

Also, each recipe (or preparation method) requires some time. A more sophisticated dish may even require two hours or more to prepare. And so, a smart cook will have fun in the process, by listening to music or talking to someone. They will not get impatient, or angry with the recipe while complaining:"Why is it taking so long?"
Also, an inexperienced cook might need even more time because they will often screw things up and attempt to make the same recipe several times, which is absolutely fine! It's all about learning and practicing.

Yet, when it comes to manifestation, so many people get impatient and cynical. I'm not judging; I used to be one of those impatient souls too! And it was my lack of patience that was blocking my positive manifestations. In fact, I would only manifest things that were making me more frustrated and impatient—such a vicious cycle!

It was when I decided to focus on the "recipes" I enjoyed while mastering them, without mindlessly attempting to speed up the "preparation method" or "cook several recipes" at once, that my manifestation journey took off.

This is my intention for writing this book. I want you to pick 1-3 "recipes" that you feel like your mind will enjoy and commit to them while mindfully declaring that from now on, you are the master of your own reality.

If you choose a method you really enjoy, just stick to it. There's no reason to switch things up unless you really feel like it. Listen to your intuition.

But before we dive into our Timeless Manifestation and Law of Attraction Secrets, I'd like to share some of the biggest lessons I've learned on my LOA journey.

It doesn't matter whether you're new to LOA or have already read hundreds of books about it. To create your dream reality successfully, you only need to pick one recipe you will enjoy.

Also, don't get discouraged by the word "Advanced" in the title. From my experience, I can tell you that *advanced* is very often much more straightforward and effective than *beginner*. Why not think of yourself as an Advanced Manifestor already? Why call yourself a beginner? I mean: you've manifested this book!

So, you're an advanced Manifestor and will get awarded with incredible, advanced techniques for you to enjoy!

Yes, I know! Our minds love playing tricks with us: *Oh come on, you're not good enough now, start with something more beginner-friendly!*
Well, this may be true in some cases.

But, when it comes to manifestation and the Law of Attraction, it's very often by setting higher goals and dreaming bigger that we can manifest our dream reality using the principles of simplicity and mindful repetition of what works for us.

So, without any further ado, let's get start

The #1 The Most Powerful Manifestation Principle That Took Me Years to Learn (+ the 3 Magical Words That Can Instantly Change Your Reality!)

Creating your own reality can be easier than you think – if you just understand its fundamental principle.

I used to believe that what happened in the past happened to me. I thought the past had the power to create my future. Even after I began reading about the Law of Attraction, I still held onto my old belief. I somehow thought that other people deserved more success and happiness, but I didn't.

I was stuck in a job that drained me. Then, I repeated the same negative pattern by chasing different business opportunities. I thought that by changing the vehicle (the way I was earning an income), I would manifest more money and abundance.

And yes, sometimes you need to change the vehicle – this can be your job or business model. However, the change must come from your authentic desire and passion for a new vehicle. Well, in my case, I was all in fear and desperation. No matter what I did, I couldn't get out of the negative cycle of negativity. I felt so depressed because other people could indeed succeed! They could try a new manifestation method and have success with it.

They could apply for a new job and get it. Or manifest it unexpectedly. They could start a new business venture and be successful. They could invest in coaching or business training. They could just follow the steps outlined in some program and create something incredible.

But I couldn't! Even though I was *doing exactly* what they did. I'm sure you can sympathize with my frustration. I thought something was wrong with me. I thought I was doing this personal development thing all for nothing.

I was learning about LOA, I was setting more intentions, I was trying to stay focused on them, and I was trying to think positive thoughts. But my self-image didn't change. You see, I still thought of myself as an average person. An average employee who works hard for peanuts. Just an average person who attempts a business opportunity from a place of lack and desperation.

So, nothing was changing for me. Yes, every now and then, I could experience a little synchronicity or a small manifestation, such as manifesting a cup of coffee or an unexpected bonus at work.

But instead of being grateful and seeing those little wins as the signs of success, my old, limited self-image saw them as signs of failure.

Look at yourself, Elena...all that time and money you spent on self-development. And what did you get? A cup of coffee and a bonus of $50? Whereas other people can manifest amazing relationships, nice houses, luxury travel, and high-paying jobs or businesses they love.

And, so my self-talk and my self-image would dictate my behaviors while creating my reality.

Then, one day, I hit rock bottom. I experienced an anxiety attack. I just cried and cried and cried. I even decided to get rid of all my self-development books and programs and "move on." *You see, Elena, you made a fool out of yourself! This stuff is not for you. It works for other people because they are smarter. But it will never work for you.*

But then, I caught myself repeating these three words – *work for you, work for you, work for you.*

I immediately stopped crying. I washed my face and looked at myself in the mirror. I could still hear these three words: *work for you, work for you, work for you.*

Then it dawned on me! Yes, it was already working for me, and I was already using the Law of Attraction. The problem was that I wasn't using it to my advantage.

Why? Because of my negative self-image backed up by the negative self-talk. My own limitations and negative beliefs about what was possible for me were blocking most, if not all, positive manifestations from my life.

Suddenly, I felt such a relief. Yes, technically, my life was still a mess. I was still recovering after an abusive relationship and a failed business that drained me.

Yet, I still felt empowered! It was as if all those beautiful and empowering self-development and law of attraction lessons suddenly made sense!
At the same time, I thought: "Hold on....you are very good at this! You can use your self-image to create your reality. The problem is that you've been using it negatively. The good news is that now you really feel and understand that this stuff works, and it can work for you if you change your self-image and decide to stop limiting yourself. "

Work for you, work for you, work for you...

You can use your self-talk and self-image to implant positive images in your mind. You can shift your identity and enjoy your new reality. Don't wait. It's already inside you. Allow it to manifest by changing who you are.

It was a very spiritual moment. And I began crying again, but this time, out of joy!

From then on, I felt like a new person, and my life was profoundly transformed. Even though technically, I was still in debt, had no real friends, and on a meager income, I felt like a different person. I felt successful. I could see myself in a different reality, doing what I love for a living, being surrounded by people who love and appreciate me, and having the time and resources to help and inspire other people.

To cut a long story short, this is how my real manifestation journey started. I decided to change my self-image. I saw myself in a different reality and began acting in alignment with my true desires. I stopped acting based on my limitations on what I thought other people wanted me to do. From then on, my life began to change. I shifted my identity and attracted a new reality.

I know you can do the same! And I feel very privileged to be sharing with you exactly what worked.

Remember these three power words: *work for you, work for you, work for you.* Keep repeating them whenever you're feeling stuck because they hold the key to your new self-image and dream reality.

"Your Past Does Not Equal to Future" – Tony Robbins

Mr. Robbins put it brilliantly. I would also add my humble words here: *you can experience your dream future right here, right now, in the present moment. The question is, what do you want it to look like?*

Exercise:

Design a vision for your dream life now and create a short mission statement for each area of your life:

My health

Example:
-I choose to eat healthy foods that give me unstoppable energy and vibrant health.

-I love foods that nourish my body.

-I'm blessed to indulge in long baths and beautiful walks in nature.

My Passion/ Purpose / Fulfillment
Example:

-I feel so grateful I found my calling in life.

-I'm even more grateful I can do my passion for a living.

-My purpose sets my soul on fire!

My relationships

Example:

-I get amazingly well with my family, friends, and the man/woman of my dreams.

-We're all happy people; we love and support each other.

-I attract high vibe people into my life.

Money/finance

Example:

-I'm open to receiving.

-I mindfully create new opportunities and new sources of income.

-Money is energy, and I'm energy; therefore, I attract money into my life.

Spirituality

Example:

-I experience unforgettable spiritual moments in my life.

- I feel loved and cared for by the Universe/God/ Higher Power.

That was the first step. Get back to it to remind yourself what's yet to come and how amazing your life can

The Indisputable Law of Self-Image

In his book *Psycho-Cybernetics*, doctor Maxwell Maltz discusses the psychology of self-image. As a plastic surgeon, he observed that it took on average two weeks for most of his patients, after their surgery was done, for their self-image to change. However, Mr. Maltz also observed that some would still feel and act as they did before the surgery unless their inner self-image changed.

He realized that there's something called the cybernetic mechanism, which means that we all have a set point for the way we see ourselves.

Suppose you see yourself as someone who can make only a certain amount of money a year. In that case, your inner resourcefulness will align with that self-image, therefore blocking true abundance.

So, how do you see yourself? If you have a look at the previous exercise, ask yourself: are you still limiting yourself? Perhaps you can re-write your vision?
My old self-image was: *yes, I would like to become an author, but writing is hard, and who would want to read my work anyway? I'm not a famous guru.*

And so, I could never concentrate on writing and felt stuck. It didn't matter what I learned about writing or publishing because I didn't feel worthy of my desires, and my reality kept reflecting that. I couldn't be consistent with my publications.

But there's also another phenomenon to understand. Some people say they really desire something, and they say how badly they want it while creating the energy of desperation. In other words, they put all their desires
on a pedestal.

It wasn't until I read the book *Reality Transurfing* by Vladim Zeland that I discovered the hidden dangers of increased importance, and how it can repel our positive manifestations.

Let's say you are getting ready to go for a date, you get obsessed with thoughts such as: *Oh, what if I get rejected? What if this man/woman doesn't like me? I want them to tell me I'm the best, or I'll feel bad!*

And so, you go on a date, and your energy, the way you talk and act, starts reflecting your self-image. You may try hard to manifest something positive, but you attach so much importance to it that, as a result, you reject it.

The Universe can sense your desperate energy. Or perhaps, you're overconfident and start bragging. Well, you may soon encounter unfavorable circumstances manifest to balance out your energy of increased self-importance.

However, if you create a positive self-image of a person who enjoys meeting new people, is friendly, loves socializing, and is a good listener, your date will go much better. When you start focusing on other people and what you can do for them, your energy is authentic, natural, and magnetic.

How many times did you want something so badly that you actually repelled it?
Negative self-image (such as too much desire, self-importance, or lack of confidence) creates resistance. It only activates the law of repulsion.

It's like chasing a cat....and it keeps running away!
In my case, I kept repelling different business opportunities because I wanted money, but at the same time, I wasn't feeling confident about money. I wanted money and success to prove myself to others. And so I unconsciously kept creating very negative energy.

The more worthy you feel inside yourself, the more magnetic you become, and manifestation becomes almost automatic.

Why do you chase money? Is it to get a sense of security or freedom? Well, you can feel these emotions right here, right now.

Focus on your inner relationships with money, love, abundance, and health- whatever it is you desire. Be that person first!

Instead of chasing things, focus on your relationship with whatever it is you want. Whatever it is you want, it's already inside you.

Finally, understand that the self-image you currently have is like a vehicle serving you on your current mission. And even if it's working for you now, at some point, you will need to let go of it and create a new one.

For example, let's say that now, you intend to manifest a freedom-based business because you want to travel the world. So, you create a self-image of someone who can live a laptop lifestyle, and your number one goal is to experience more travel. You join different digital nomad communities and train your mind to look for work or business opportunities that align with your travel goals.

But, maybe after four years of a non-stop digital nomad lifestyle, you decide to settle down. You enjoyed your travels but now feel like slowing down a bit. You want to buy a house and start a family. You no longer wish to be a digital nomad. Instead, you feel like starting a local business and creating job opportunities for your local community.

It's all about understanding who you truly are, right here and right now. Everything is in constant flow. Our energy and priorities can always change. The mistake that so many people make is that they get stuck in their old self-image and old desires that are no longer authentic. It's all about understanding when to let go of the old and embrace the new.

If you have a big dream that you intend to manifest and feel like something is blocking you, chances are it's your old self-image.

For example, when I was getting started on my writing journey, I got stuck in my old self-image of someone who could not finish what they start and gets burned out quickly. But, I knew I had a mission I wanted to accomplish. I knew I wanted to write to raise the vibration of the planet. And so, in alignment with my mission, I had to let go of my old-self image. Instead, I had to create a self-image of an organized and prolific writer who always finishes what they start. In other words, to fulfill my mission, I had to embrace my inner leadership and responsibility.

What is your old-self image? Is it still helpful? If not, create a new self-image that aligns with your current mission! The following pages will inspire you to unleash your hidden manifestation powers in alignment with your true, authentic desires!

Manifestation Secrets Demystified

Each secret will help you learn a practical law of attraction or manifestation principle or technique. Some secrets will challenge your way of thinking, feeling, or acting. Stick to the secrets that really resonate with you and start mindfully applying them to watch your life transform as you've always wanted!

Secret#1 The Number One Question You Absolutely Can't Ignore

Before you even commence on your manifestation journey, you need to do a quick energy check. Luckily, no complicated rituals are required. You simply need to ask yourself, from what place are you intending to manifest?

If it's from a place of seeking approval and validation from others, you have some work to do! No, I don't want to scare you or make you feel bad about yourself. You should be glad you are discovering it now before it's too late.

So what exactly am I implying? Well, are you stuck on a hamster wheel? Just chasing, chasing, and chasing? And do you feel worthy of manifesting your desires, even before they appear in your reality?

For example, if your main motivations focus on chasing validation and approval, you will feel stuck, no matter what you manifest. You've probably heard many stories of famous people and celebrities who had it all, money, fame, and relationships with other well-known individuals. Yet, they still felt unhappy or stuck, often resorting to drugs to ease their inner pain.

Another problem with seeking approval is that you may feel tempted to start manifesting goals that are not even yours, to begin with. I have been there so many times! If you have read more of my books in this series, you probably already know my story. If you didn't then, the quick summary of Elena's story is that she spent years chasing and trying to manifest goals that weren't even hers. It took her years of personal development and spirituality work to dive deeper and understand what was really going on. One of the biggest catalysts on her journey was discovering Vladim Zeland's work and reading his book *Reality Transurfing*. After applying his teachings, Elena fully understood that the number one secret to manifesting is to make sure the goal you want to accomplish is genuinely yours.

OK, enough writing about myself in the third person! And back to the main topic – your authentic manifestation energy.

This concept is so important to understand because it can save you years of mindless chasing while stuck on a hamster wheel.

Another thing to keep in mind is that all the entities around you (when I say "entities," I mean both people and the Universe, or any spiritual beings you choose to believe in) can feel your personal energy. If all your actions and thoughts are driven by the need to get validation from others, the energy you create lacks authentic confidence and conviction. No wonder it's hard to manifest what you want. Those around you can feel your inner motives, and the message they receive is:*" Oh OK, he or she wants to get my approval, but they don't approve themselves and lack confidence. "*

Even if you are not into energy stuff, the "stuck on a hamster wheel" concept can also be explained without diving into energy or spirituality concepts.

Let's say a person wants to manifest a better job with a better salary, only because they want others to praise them. So, they go to job interviews. But, they are so self-absorbed that they aren't even able to clearly communicate their value, so they never do well in job interviews. Even if they somehow get their dream job, they are still in the mindset of "I am not good enough" and find a way to sabotage their success or feel stuck again. Yes, they will get some appreciation and feel good about it. But, whenever achievement stops, they will feel bad about themselves: *OMG, nobody is praising me anymore, I'm probably not good enough or doing something wrong.*

In contrast, a person who embraces their true, authentic self-love and seeks a better job because they are passionate about pursuing a new career or working for a specific company can think and act from a place of laser focus. They already feel good and validated within themselves. So they can use all their mental energy to research the company they want to work for and present their value to potential employers in a way that's easy to understand. They don't stress out about the final outcome because they know that even if they don't get their dream job now, they are already validated. Each attempt to seek professional improvement brings them closer to manifesting their dreams whenever the timing is right.

However, a person who wants to manifest because they seek approval and validation might take any rejection very personally: *"Oh no, now they will not love me! I'm not good enough. I should probably try harder."*

Whereas the right question should be: are you even trying to manifest your own goals? And do you want to achieve them because they are in alignment with who you really are? Or is it because you want somebody to approve you?

You can be in charge of how people around you and the Universe respond to you. It starts with self-honesty. You can choose to embody the energy of natural confidence and conviction now.

I like to use the term "natural confidence" or "authentic confidence" because trying to be more confident can be tricky as well. We often chase confidence thinking it's something we can demonstrate by trying to speak like an authority or making others follow us.

I used to work with quite a few pretty famous online influencers. And let me tell you this- many of them confided in me that they felt tired of acting on social media. It's like putting on a mask to convey a specific image of artificial confidence. So that their followers on social media can get inspired. But then, what happens behind the scenes? Are they the same people on YouTube or Instagram as they are in real life?

One influencer told me that creating a half an hour video felt very painful for her because she had to keep on a mask, which turned out to be exhausting in the long run.

I advised her to be authentic instead. If you choose to lead and influence people, the best long-term strategy is to connect with them on a deeper level. And how can you connect with someone if you can't even connect with yourself by being honest about who you are?

People like honest and real people. So, natural and authentic confidence is the only way to manifest lasting success and personal and professional relationships.

So, get rid of the concept of: "I need to look like I'm confident, and so I should imitate people who are famous for being confident."

Stop *shoulding* yourself! Embrace your uniqueness and make it shine as never before!

What really works is being *you*. Be kind to yourself and make peace with yourself. Accept who you are and embody your truth. This is the natural and authentic confidence – the only way to get rid of the energy of desperation.

So stop chasing validation, approval, and success. Yes, the feeling of significance can help you feel better, but it will be very short-term. You tell yourself that the more you do something, whether it's getting more followers, more readers, more bestselling book badges, more high-ticket clients, or more appreciation from your boss or family – the more you will love yourself.

However, what can happen is that when you get to your goal, you will not feel happy. Instead, you will want more followers, bestselling badges, or appreciation.

The fantasies of the mind love fake and fleeting feelings of significance. However, from my experience, the best fantasy is the one you create through your heart, right here and right now. You can choose to love yourself and feel validated and appreciated right here, right now.

There is nothing wrong with desiring to manifest success, money, or moving up your career ladder. But before you begin, release the need to control everyone and everything around you.

Simultaneously, if your current desires are centered around manifesting love and extraordinary relationships because you are not feeling love from within you and want others to love you first, you need to be careful not to activate the Law of Repulsion.

Whatever your manifestation goal is, promise yourself right here and right now that you already embody it and feel absolutely at peace with it. Validate and approve yourself- all you need is a simple decision and mindset shift. Feel abundant with feelings of love, positivity, and harmony, and you will become a magnet for people, circumstances, and energies that want to help you on your journey.

Exercise:

Have a look at your previous goals and accomplishments. What was your why? Did you desire significance, approval, and validation?

Was it hard to manifest your desires?

How did others respond to your energy?

What about your current goals and manifestations? Can you already feel whole and complete? Can you embody the energy of love, harmony, peace, and positivity right here and right now?

Important – don't judge yourself when doing this exercise. It's all about learning! We all catch ourselves, "making mistakes" every now and then. But this is how we learn. When you realize you can change something in your way of thinking and acting, be grateful because you are your best teacher. Now you know what not to do, which is a significant step to move forward!

Secret#2 Trying to Re-Program Your Subconscious Mind? Discover Why It Might NOT Work Unless You De-Program It First

Do you know how to make your subconscious mind listen to you? Can you actually imprint your authentic desires and use the power of your subconscious mind to guide you?

Or do you tend to fall back to your old patterns?

We all want something, but, in most cases, we were programmed and conditioned to get something different. At the same time, wanting something is not very helpful because you send a message to the Universe that you don't have it.

The challenge is how to get to the right place of *being* and stop fighting with ourselves. The biggest battle is the one we experience within ourselves as we keep on *wanting* while experiencing inner resistance amplified by rejection from the world.

This section might be a bit difficult to comprehend, especially if you're new to the subconscious or unconscious mind concepts, so if needed, read it several times. As Bob Proctor says, it's all about repetition. And he's well known for reading the same book - *Think and Grow Rich* every day.

OK, so let's make your subconscious mind work for you! It doesn't have to be hard. You just need to understand the basics.

When you are presented with a new idea, it's just an idea because there is no proof, whether such an idea feels good or bad, empowering or dangerous.

But when you start creating any proof around it, based on your experiences, observations, past hurts, or successes, it becomes a belief, which can be negative or positive. In other words, your belief can be limiting or empowering.

For example, you start a YouTube channel, and it's not growing as fast as you imagined. You research other people's channels, and you say to yourself: *Oh, they have more followers, they are more successful. I will never be like them.*

Of course, for some reason, you don't focus on the fact that other channels have been in the game for many, many years, and they all started exactly the way you did, if not less successful!

Then some troll posts a negative comment on your videos, and you form a belief that your channel sucks. You are sure it's because of your ethnicity, lack of college degree, or something else such as your hair, teeth, or accent.

Then, your thought is backed up by a negative feeling, and now you are very successfully *not* manifesting your desires. I will add this- as humans, we are real experts in creating negative beliefs.

We are successfully creating what we don't want while moving away from our goals.

But this is where the true empowerment can take place (if you allow it!). This is the real secret behind the secret!

You are not broken. There is nothing wrong with you. You are a successful manifestor, no matter what results you get from your efforts. You are already very talented at creating firm beliefs by combining your thoughts with certain feelings. Your mind and body know how to manifest.

For me, this was the most significant *aha* moment on my self-improvement journey. I asked myself- *what if I could positively use my natural powers? What if I used my senses, energies, thoughts, and feelings, in a way that is positive and aligns with my goals?*

So, let me repeat, whatever "bad results" you have manifested in your life so far, give yourself some credit because you are just very talented at using your mind to create your reality. You can manifest! So now, get excited because you can use the exact same system you have been using your entire life but in a consciously positive and empowering way.

Oh, there will be some side effects to this, so please be warned! One of them is that you will feel more energized. Yes, you will have more energy to do what you love. It will be natural energy. You will no longer need to rely on coffee to get going.

No, I'm not going mad. What you'are reading right here and right now is one of the biggest secrets to manifestation, lifestyle design, or reality creation. Whatever you want to call it.

OK, so you realize you are not broken, and nothing is wrong with you. You know you have been negatively using your inner manifestation system. Perhaps you even got addicted to your old story? Feeling like there is something wrong with you, some heavy dark energies made a pact to get you!

But now, you are making a conscious effort to use your inner manifestation system in a way that aligns with your desires. You realize you were addicted to worrying, stress, and criticism. You decide to quit negativity and gradually start experiencing more energy.

But what happens then? Your subconscious mind was programmed for the negative for so many years. And now, you have more energy to do the things you love. All the time and energy you save on stress, worry, anger, or replaying some gloomy scenes from the past...what are you going to do with this time and energy?

This is when many people self-sabotage and get back to old patterns.

Hey, let's call this old buddy and gossip. Let's scroll on social media and worry we are not good enough. Yes, I know, I know. I was supposed to start my own inspirational Instagram page.

And I feel like I could, with all this free time and energy. But...I'm still addicted to my old, negative patterns!

Once again, this is a great talent and skill. So, if you've ever experienced any forms of self-sabotage before, once again, give yourself some credit. You are very good at this. And as a recovering *self-sabotage-holic* (I was the queen of *self-sabotage-holism*, probably one of the most talented ever!) I definitely applaud you!

And once again, It's not my intention to make you feel bad or scared. I want you to feel relaxed and playful, knowing that your inner manifestation system works, and it works very well!

Now you also know the side effects of changing your inner patterns and habits. You might experience more time and energy, and your subconscious mind might start rebelling, saying: "Hey, what are we going to do with all this extra time and energy?"

Once again, as one of the most skilled manifestation experts on this planet, you need to make a choice. Changing your subconscious mind by choosing different thoughts, feelings, and actions may feel uncomfortable.

It's like trying to go on a healthy diet. When you first get started, you feel very tempted to reverse back to your old patterns. Your subconscious mind is just waiting to demonstrate the superiority of your old negative eating patterns and programs.

But you can always choose and start a nice, peaceful dialog with your subconscious mind, using this template:

I used to believe that my old limiting belief was true.

And I thank you, my deep inner mind (or my subconscious mind), for holding on to this belief. Thank you, thank you, thank you. It was so much fun back then.

But NOW, I choose a new belief because I'm a new person.

Use this template as an exercise to start a dialog with your subconscious mind.

But please be warned, you might also be tempted to use your well-deserved title of being the world's leading expert of self-sabotage and negative thoughts. So, what do you choose?

Can you start associating positive thoughts, feelings, and actions with fun? Will you take the challenge of becoming the world's leading expert in the field of positive thinking and acting? Or perhaps you still hold onto your old self-image of negativity, feeling so addicted to it. I mean, you worked very hard. You put so much effort into creating long-lasting negative patterns and habits. You designed a very smart diet for your mind; a diet of stress, worry, anger, sadness. You were extremely successful with this diet for so many years. You stuck with it, without any cheat days! Well done!

And now what? Something new? Changing your mind? Losing your well-deserved achievement of becoming an expert in the field of worry and creating negative movies in your mind?

If you're laughing while reading this- keep laughing because it puts you in a higher vibration and energized state of being. I don't know about you, but I prefer laughter to self-guilt or self-blame. I've been there as well. I will brag about my "credentials" again; I used to be a Self-Guilt Queen. In fact, I was one of the world's leading specialists in the field of self-blame, and I took my title very seriously, always looking for new ways to torture myself with what "I did wrong and what I should have done instead".

If you are not laughing, then no worries, I understand that not everyone gets my sense of humor, and we will get very serious in just a minute!

I see these patterns all the time amongst people who study self-development. They learn a new concept or technique and discover something about themselves. And, very often, their mind starts playing tricks on them, such as: "Oh my God. Look at you! What have you done? You're such a fool. You were doing it all wrong until now! Why didn't you learn about it earlier? Imagine how your life would be different if you had only studied this book earlier. You wasted so many years! And now, look at you!"

The secrets of the world's leading self-guilt trip authorities might be the next book in the series!

But really, stop being so serious and stop *shoulding* yourself. Whenever I get a negative thought or catch myself re-playing some cynical movie from the past or even an imaginary movie of what can go wrong, I just say to myself: "Come on, Elena, this was your old job. In that job, you were an expert on worry, doubts, and fear. But now you're working a different job, remember? Well, it's kind of the same job, but a different department. So yea, keep playing movies, but make them nice and be kind to yourself. Remember? You can be the world's leading expert of positive thinking!"

This is the moment when you get out of your self-imposed negative trance and allow yourself to wake up! Now you can make a conscious decision to use your inner talents of creating thoughts and emotions to empower and motivate you, rather than get you off track and make you feel unworthy.

Whenever you get a thought and strong emotions are there, you make it into a firm belief (positive and negative). Then, you start looking for proof to confirm your new belief and align it with your insecurities.

Example:

-*Oh, I can't be successful because I am a woman*

-*I don't have money to invest in marketing*

-I can't be a motivational speaker because of my accent

-I can't do this, because nobody in my town is doing it

Then, most people feel pain and resistance and try affirmations such as: "I am rich, successful, confident," but from a lack and negativity. Their state of being is very contracted. They might feel angry or frustrated and start reciting some affirmations while hoping for the best.

While these techniques can work, they are just techniques. You try to work hard to change what you believe, or in other words, you can try to re-program yourself by adding some positive techniques while still in a negative state. My personal opinion is that it's always better than not doing anything at all and just complaining.

But what's more useful is embracing the principle of de-programming yourself first! Remember that any technique such as affirmation is just an extension of a timeless manifestation principles rooted in your self-image. In my books, I always underline the concept of fully understanding and integrating the manifestation principles first, such as permanently shifting your mindset and energy. Living by timeless manifestation principles such as what is share in this book, will give you much better results than merely chasing the latest manifestation "hack", without ever attempting to go deeper and working on your mindset and energy.

I don't know about you, but I like results. I don't like trying something half-heartedly while hoping for the best. I like to have a holistic system I can repeatedly use to get better results and keep manifesting the new levels of whatever reality I desire to create for myself.

Before infusing yourself with genuine positivity, you need to face your inner demons and release them. It's like the peeling for the mind and soul. Imagine you want to get some new furniture. Well, first, you will probably get rid of the old one, right? Unless you want to end up in a crammed apartment.

Yet, so many people love cramming their minds with whatever new hack they can find about LOA. And yes, whatever they do, they are very good at it.

Extremely talented Mind Cramming experts! Give them some credit!

You feel bad? Just recite a random affirmation. Stay crammed and confused. *Maybe this will work. I don't know. I just hope. Whatever the wind is, I will fly there.*

You can try hard to change what you believe. But you can also destroy a belief and step into a new one while using your mind to create evidence that it will work for you.

Remember a person who wanted to start a YouTube channel? They worked very hard to find the evidence they couldn't do it.

They did their research that confirmed other content creators were successful and had a ton of subscribers.

Well, but how about researching their humble beginnings? Or how about creating a list stating the reasons why you can be successful? Or focusing on your audience and serving it the best you can by creating new content? How about using your extraordinary talent and expertise to play movies in your mind, but in a more empowering way, while truly feeling your success and acting as if you were successful (because you already are! Remember there is no need to prove anything).

If you enter such an empowered state of being, you will create and upload your videos like crazy.

While this is just an example, whatever you do, you can create positive proof and evidence to make your inner manifestation system work for you, not against you.

I'm using this methodology to keep writing new books! In fact, I've been using my inner system for years. However, at first, I was in my old identity as an international expert on worry, and limiting beliefs. So, I would write a book and feel scared. The movie I kept playing in my mind was extremely negative. In fact, I won several well-acclaimed awards because of my abilities to create negative movies in my mind. I felt anxious and even buried my dreams for a while. Oh, boy, was I good at making those movies back then. But now, when I talk about it, it just seems funny.

For those of you superstitious manifestors who fear that the mere fact of mentioning your old negative patterns will make them manifest and doom you for life, please relax!

Yes, I love positivity, but I'm no fan of toxic positivity. I don't subscribe to burning your head in the sand, pretending it's always so good. No, my friend, you need to be proactive. Face your negative thoughts, be aware of them. Realize they are blocking you on many levels, and make a decision to erase them. Get rid of the old tape, disk, or program and then create a new one. And yes, you will still remember the old negative one, but it will no longer affect you. It will seem a bit unreal, funny, or even grotesque.

Doing affirmations or any other technique is not effective at all if done from a place of resistance.

Doing and being are two different states. It's not that much about what you do. It's about who you are or who you become. What is the intention that you have? Are you doing affirmations from a place of resistance? Whatever you tell yourself (while in a position of resistance, need, and stress) affirms what you don't have.

First, be in a relaxed state. Any state of relaxation helps erase resistance while making your subconscious mind prone to new, empowering suggestions.

The real question is: why do you want to manifest success? To move towards something that excites you, or to get far away from what you hate? The second option automatically implies that your focus is still on what you don't want, which may activate some old, negative programs.

You need to take meaningful and aligned action from a place of emptiness and relaxation. By entering a relaxed state of being, you are no longer aligned with old programs and energies that are holding you back. In other words- you de-program yourself before allowing any new programs in.

Let's say a person who is a business owner is feeling frustrated because they are not attracting enough clients. And suddenly one of their long-term clients decides to ask for a refund! Needless to say, the business owner feels very angry and sad. They keep thinking: *"why does this always happen to me? I work so hard! How could they do this to me?"*

And then, they try to recite several affirmations, such as:

" Oh, but I'm rich, my clients love me."

Which makes them feel even worse because they can feel a massive gap between where they are now and where they want to be. There's a big split between what they affirm and how they actually feel, think, and act.

What they could do instead is to relax for a few minutes (a few deep breaths can really do the trick) and then write down why they feel grateful for the client who just asked for a refund.

For example: *even though they decided to stop using our services, we really enjoyed working together for many years, and now at least I know the type of clients I want to work with. Maybe, I can ask them for honest feedback as to why they decided to stop using our services and use it to improve my business?*

Such a mental and energetic switch can take place in less than 5 minutes. Then, your mind will start looking for more positive things about this seemingly "negative" situation. And yes, after you've pressed that positivity button in your deep inner mind, you can start using your affirmations or visualizations. You can visualize your bank account or emails from happy clients. You can affirm: *I'm on my way, I'm in the process of transforming my business, I love it, it's so much fun!*

Whatever affirmations (or visualizations) you use, confirm them every day by staying focused on your progress and deep gratitude for everyone and everything around you.

For example, a business owner may feel frustrated because they didn't reach enough clients. At the same time, they can choose to feel grateful for the clients that already enrolled in their programs. They can keep affirming: "*if one person got interested in my services, I'm sure that soon I will have tens, hundreds, or even thousands of interested prospects and clients. I'm on my way!*"

Instead of thinking: *Oh, this will not work, I just suck.* While mindlessly affirming: *I'm a millionaire!*

You want to manifest a healthy body and weight loss? Your original goal was to lose 10 pounds. And you lost 2 pounds. Well, you can choose to complain about the fact that it's taking too long and you still have 8 pounds to lose, and it will probably never work for you anyway because of your genetics, your job, or your spouse. Or you can focus on the fact that you've already lost 2 pounds, and your body knows exactly how much time it needs to lose weight effectively and permanently. For now, why not enjoy the process of learning more about healthy living while using it as an opportunity to transform your life?

Why focus on what is not working? You can focus on what is working- this is the best affirmation and one of the most vital signals you can send to the Universe.

Be your affirmations.

Also, affirmations are not only about what you say. They are also about what you do and what you decide to embody as you go through your daily activities.

The biggest mistake that I see people in the LOA community make is focusing on some new method or technique without genuinely understanding its basic principles.

They may know many different manifestation methods, but since they don't fully understand the principles, they are just paying lip service while mindlessly reciting some affirmations. Maybe it will work, perhaps not. Who knows?

I don't know about you, but I want results.

Whatever it is that you do, always strive to differentiate between timeless principles and on-and-off tactics. For example, many online entrepreneurs get lost in a zillion of tactics such as: *shall I do a podcast, or run Facebook ads, or write blogs?* In reality, all these marketing techniques can work, but the main principle is- is there a market for what you do? Can you communicate your value? And who do you want to attract?

A person who wants to lose weight and live a healthy lifestyle can also get lost in zillions of different diets and meal plans. And they can all be helpful, but people must first embrace the basic principles: *treat your body like a temple and nourish it with real, nutritious food. Move your body, burn some calories, feel energized!*

If you have tried manifesting before using a zillion of tactics, it's time to explore your inner state. I'm pretty sure you already understand the importance of focusing on the positive. I'm all for positivity. But, getting rid of negativity is also essential. You can have the best affirmations in the world, but you will only amplify negativity and magnify what you don't have if you use them while in a negative state.

Consciously train your mind to affirm your little wins as much as you can! Someone smiles at you? Wow, it's because your energy is improving! Have you just made your first sale in your business? Well, it's just the beginning! What about that job interview? Perfect! You're in the right vibration already!

One of the best affirmations you can embrace is looking for confirmations and positive evidence. Give yourself more credit because you are already manifesting your dreams! It's only getting better and better.

Even if something doesn't go your way, you can choose to use it to your advantage. Maybe the Universe wants to test you?

Remember that you can't get rejected. You can only get re-directed. Everything is unfolding just like it should!

Exercise

1.What is your goal or desire you wish to manifest?

Describe all the details using the present tense, as if you already had it.

2. Enter a relaxed and fun state by listening to your favorite song, dancing around, and taking a few deep breaths.

3.Now, have a look at your current reality and everyday activities. What signals are you getting from the Universe? Train your mind to look for as many positive confirmations as you possibly can.

4. When you wake up and go to bed, talk to yourself kindly and keep reminding yourself of all the beautiful things you are already receiving and why you are more than worthy of manifesting all your desires.

Let's say you want to "program yourself" to be a full-time entrepreneur, and this week you had a potential client reaching out to you. Whenever a client reaches out to you for your services, this actually signals your progress! Make sure you appreciate that and give yourself a well-deserved pat on the back.

"Everything is unfolding just like it should; I'm moving forward."

What you're actually doing is crossing the threshold from an opinion to a firm, positive belief because when you show yourself confirmation, your RAS (Reticular Activating System) filters out for things that actually lead to your goal.

So, start to notice more of what is working fine and, if needed, address what is not working from a positive standpoint to improve yourself. You don't fail. You succeed, or you learn!

Secret #3 The Missing Links between Desire and Aligned Action (and the Best Manifestation Shortcut)

As we have already stated: Non-neediness is one of the primary keys to successful and truly happy manifestations.

Yes, you want embody your deep inner faith that you will be successful because you already are successful.

Always remember that your success doesn't need to rely on some external factor. You are already successful. You have already manifested many amazing things, no matter what you have or don't have!

Your mind is continuously making evaluations by asking questions, and it's up to you to make it work in your favor.

One of the biggest lessons I've learned from Tony Robbins is that if we change and empower our questions, we make better and more empowering decisions and choices. In other words- when you change the way you see the world, you change the world.

Now, here's some good news...everybody can manifest and use their mind to create their reality. Whether they are getting the results they actually want is a different story. Most people never wake up, and therefore don't even attempt to take full ownership of their minds.

They set a goal and have a little bit of faith in it in the beginning. But then, they allow some negative thoughts and beliefs to take over. Instead of focusing on what could go well, they focus on what could go wrong. In alignment with their negative thoughts, they take negative actions and never manifest their true desires.

The way it works is best described by Napoleon Hill's Triangle of *Desire-Faith-Action*. To manifest successfully, you need a positive desire backed up with positive faith and action. So many people never get to manifest their desires because they don't take consistent positive action. And the reason why they don't take positive action is that they begin doubting themselves, which leads to losing faith. They start doubting because they don't use their mind to ask empowering positive questions. These questions are the missing link in the desire-faith-and-action triangle.

While some might say that empowering questions are only needed to create faith and that faith automatically leads to action, I'd venture to say that we need empowering questions all the time because they also lead to empowering actions.

There are many ways to create empowering questions that fully support your manifestation journey. However, my favorite method to develop as many empowering questions as you need to is through Identity Shifting.

First, you need to come up with an exciting vision for your life. What do you desire to manifest? And who are you in that vision?

What are your thoughts, feelings, and actions? This is the New You or the 2.0 version of You.

To come up with some genuinely empowering questions, start thinking just like your new 2.0 version does.

I used to feel stuck in my desire to become a writer. But I could never take consistent actions to support my vision. I was more like a wannabee, haha. And so, years would pass, I would keep myself busy with other "goals," and I simply wasn't consistent with writing new books.

So, I created a new vision for my life. I said to myself: *"OK, Elena, you are a super creative writer. You are a serial author. You are a writing machine."*

I even visualized my readers visiting me at my home and literally requesting me to write more.

They would even make me tea and coffee and cook my meals. It was a funny, grotesque vision, and it worked very well for me. It's up to you if you decide to use humor in your visualizations.

I also imagined I had deadlines and that instead of being self-employed, I was hired by some secret love-based mindset agents. In that vision, my only job was to write as much as possible because it was a part of the Positivity Mission I was on with other secret agents.

So, I began asking myself empowering questions: *how would my new 2.0 version think? What questions would they ask?*

My old self was in a negative mindset, asking negative questions such as:

-why can't I grow my audience? I guess I will never be successful.

-why can other authors write so fast and I can't? I guess I should just quit before I make a fool out of myself.

-what if some of my friends and family find my work and don't like it? Because you know, I still remember when I wrote my first poem as a teen, and they just laughed at it.

However, my new self knows how to ask empowering questions such as:

-I wonder how it would feel to get emails from happy readers who appreciate my work?

-Can I write a book to help at least 1 person manifest their desires? And what if I could help 10, 100, or even 1000 people? I mean, other authors can do it. So let's keep writing!

-If I had a mailing list of readers, what kind of emails would I send? Would I share some personal stories? Would I ask for feedback? Would they feel excited to get some excerpts from my new books?

Trust me, it works every time. Whenever you use your mind to create empowering questions, your faith goes to the next level, and you take positive action that feels so aligned that you no longer feel like you "have to motivate and discipline yourself to work harder." You simply embody your desire, faith, and goals by already *being* the person who manifests effortlessly.

Exercise

I strongly recommend you take a little break from reading this book and grab yourself a nice cup of coffee or tea. Relax and write down (in detail):

-Your dream reality (from the first person).

For example:

I am a high-end coach. I'm so excited to be working with all those celebrities, actors, entrepreneurs, and even other coaches. It's such a privilege to help them transform their mindsets to do better in their careers while providing entertainment and transformation to other people. I love my mission!

-Your new, empowering questions (that your new, 2.0 version asks), for example:

What would it feel like to do my own seminars? How would I feel when talking in front of hundreds of people?

Instead of: *why can't I grow my YouTube audience? I guess nobody is interested in what I do. Let's watch Netflix instead! I feel so stupid. Who do I think I was? I could never become a high-end coach. I mean, why would those famous people want to hire me anyway?*

Please note, sometimes a question may seem a bit negative but can be used for positive or growth purposes.

For example, you can ask yourself:

Why can't I grow my YouTube audience? – but from a place of curiosity and playfulness.

Imagine you are a LOA detective on a mission to solve a case! You're like Sherlock Holmes of Manifestation.

Hmmm...let's see. Perhaps it's because you are not uploading enough videos? Or maybe the titles don't resonate with your audience? Or perhaps you could do better thumbnails? Or perhaps it would be a good idea to work with a coach who could improve your communication skills? Or perhaps it's keyword optimization? Or your camera and lightning or audio quality?

Whatever the reason is, there is no place for negativity here because we are solving a very important case while having fun and learning.

Another great (and extremely vibration-raising) exercise you can do is imagine you've already manifested your goal. Let's stick to our previous example of a high-end coach.

So now, you are giving a speech at some incredible, high-vibe seminar. You can see all your role models and mentors sitting in the audience, listening to your story while nodding and smiling. Many find your speech inspiring and breathtaking.

In that speech, you share what it took to be successful and all the obstacles you had to overcome, and how grateful you feel for them now because they made you who you are today!

And remember, you are always in control. We all get bombarded with negative thoughts because our brain has only one goal. It wants to keep us safe. I, too, get negative thoughts such as:

Oh, what if someone doesn't like my work?

Then, I catch myself getting off track and immediately say to myself: *"cancel-cancel- cancel."* I immediately ask myself:

Hmm, what if I publish this book and people like it? What if they post a positive review? And, it's not even about reviews. What if they actually apply my techniques, use them to transform their lives, and then start helping other people too?

Both positivity and negativity are infectious. The levels of effort required to spread negativity are the same as the efforts needed to spread positivity. It's just a question of getting used to embodying positivity and making it your lifestyle. Embodying positivity while looking for confirmations of what is already working in your favor is the best affirmation (and visualization) you could create! Stay focused on the process.

So why not choose positivity and make it your default state?

If you're looking for an actual method to apply after reading this book, then be sure to use empowering questions and start writing them down. Be consistent, do it every day. Even one empowering question a day can be a missing piece to your manifestation journey and can really supercharge your efforts!

You can also combine empowering questions with gratitude. First, write down a few things you are grateful for right now in your current reality to really get in a good vibe. Then, write down a few things you are thankful for. Things that you know already exist in your new reality (in other words, something you haven't manifested yet, but are already grateful for). Finally, write down at least one empowering question.

Don't get stuck where so many people do. You need positive desire, faith, and action – and the best way to consistently keep fueling all three is with empowering questions!

Secret #4 Manifest Faster By Slowing Down! (The #1 Thing to Learn from Mindful Manifestors)

Some days you may start experiencing impatience. *Why is it taking so long? What can I do to manifest faster? Maybe I need to get a new manifestation skill? Or perhaps this method isn't for me?*

It's absolutely normal to start experiencing impatience every now and then. I've been there too! And what I've learned is that whenever you feel impatient, you have two choices. You can push harder and start obsessing about your goals, while experiencing anxiety.

Or, you can use your impatience as a signal from the Universe that you need to relax and let go a bit! Trust me when I say this- the second option works much better!

As an impatient manifestor, you may feel tempted to end up with the first option while turning your impatience into anxiety and unhealthy obsession.

But, in nature, everything needs time. And you need to let go and relax. Be grateful that your mind is sending you all those amazing signals through the feelings of impatience, and schedule some time for self-care to allow your mind to stop focusing on your goals so that it can relax and rejuvenate. My favorite way of doing so is by incorporating simple mindfulness techniques into my life.

You can enjoy the moment and allow yourself to let go of small, gradual changes in life, even if you're busy. Mindfulness doesn't have to be complicated. It's not about levitating over your bed; it's about tuning in with your senses. Embracing a mindful lifestyle will allow you to concentrate and work better while enjoying all the little things in your life and reducing anxious states.

"To let go means to give up coercing, resisting, or struggling, in exchange for something more powerful and wholesome which comes out of allowing things to be as they are without getting caught up in your attraction to or rejection of them, in the intrinsic stickiness of wanting, of liking and disliking. Just watch this moment without trying to change it at all. What is happening? What do you feel? What do you see? What do you hear?" - by Jon Kabat-Zinn

Mindfulness Meditation is all about perceiving, concentrating, observing, and cultivating the present moment. It's one of the best ways to enter a relaxed state while raising your vibration! Below are my favorite mindfulness techniques- feel free to choose the ones you like and start practicing them to erase impatient and anxious states. After all, you don't want to be a stressed-out manifestor. Instead, you want to experience peace, happiness, and relaxation while sending out a positive vibration to the Universe- you feel calm knowing everything is unfolding just like it should, and you choose to enjoy the present moment.

Mindful Anchor Exercise

Keep your attention focused on any object of your choice for a few minutes or more. It can be a statue, a picture, a tree, a flower, or a candle. Set the alarm to give yourself a few minutes of peace.

Fall in Love with Breathing

Breathe in and out several times. Find out where you feel your breath – is it your chest, stomach, rib cage, nose, mouth, or throat? What happens, and what sensations do you experience after changing the duration of your breath (making it longer or shorter)? Don't judge yourself. Whatever it is, let it be and embrace curiosity. This will allow you to tune into your body and mind and read whatever signal you get from them quickly and effortlessly!

Ice cube meditation.

To do this mindfulness exercise, simply hold an ice cube in your hand until it melts. Let the melted ice spill onto your lap or on the table. Observe your sensations and feelings. Do you feel discomfort? Do you feel like quitting? Mindfully register whatever happens in your body.

Digital detox

When do you usually feel tempted to check your phone? What are your emotional triggers that make you scroll on social media or check your email? Is it really necessary? Analyze if you do it before you get out of bed, during meals, while talking to someone else, maybe on the bus? Allow yourself to spend a day without your phone. Plan ahead by writing down all the impulses that make you check your phone. Is it sadness? Impatience? Boredom? What if, instead of checking your phone, you could meditate or do a simple mindfulness exercise, or go for a short walk?

Curious Walking

Go on a mindful walk. It can be in your local park or any open space in nature. Explore the place without any purpose. Begin by feeling the sensation of your feet stepping on and off the ground. Allow your mind to register everything you see and feel. When your thoughts drift in a different direction, try to get your attention back on your feet, as well as the air you breathe and the sounds you hear.

Mindful Tea or Coffe Break

Make yourself a cup of your favorite tea or coffee. Breathe in the scent. Savor the flavor. Feel the temperature and mindfully enjoy it!

Whenever your mind drifts, and you catch yourself stressing out about your everyday concerns, pay attention to different parts of your body: your feet, ankles, legs, hips, hands, etc. Feel how you fill your lungs with air and imagine that you bring that breath to every part of your body. Then, carry on sipping your tea or coffee! If you don't have the time to meditate for hours, you can choose to turn your tea or coffee breaks into mini mindfulness meditations while letting go of stress, worry, and impatience.

Simple Seated Meditation

Sit down in a comfortable position. Put your hands on your knees, palms down, or put one hand on the other. Imagine that your head is a helium balloon. Let it rise naturally and stretch your spine. Lean back and forth a few times until you find the midpoint of balance.

Focus on your breathing. Make sure your mind doesn't wander. If you notice that you have lost concentration, come back. No judgment here!

Simple Sound Meditation

Start by noticing the sounds in your body, the sounds in the room you are in, the sounds in the building, and finally, the sounds outside. Let the sounds sink in instead of struggling to capture them. Listen mindfully. Keep it up for about ten more minutes.

When you are ready, draw attention from outside sounds to your thoughts. Watch how thoughts arise and go. As soon as you notice that your attention becomes entangled in a thread of ideas, take a step back calmly, away from your thoughts, and return to observe them in the distance, as much as you can.

As you can see, mindfulness is a lifestyle choice, and it doesn't have to be about long or complicated rituals. It's all about understanding how to observe whatever happens around and inside you. Become an observer of your reality and take joy in being able to be a part of it.

Promise yourself to appreciate the present moment and feel good about it because it's thanks to living and fully being in the present moment that you can let go of past hurts and mindfully create a fantastic future.

Secret#5 Does Your Environment Block Your Manifestations? (Feng Shui It Up to Show the Universe You are Ready to Receive!)

Have a closer look at your home and office. Does your environment affirm your desires?

For example, if your workspace is cluttered, you may find yourself feeling stuck in your professional life, not manifesting your career goals successfully.

If you want to attract more money and abundance into your life, does your wallet reflect your desires? For example, if your wallet is old and full of clutter, such as some old receipts, no wonder it's getting harder and harder to manifest more money into your life.

What about your handbag, purse, backpack or car? Are they too filled with objects you no longer need? What about those old papers and receipts?

Do you often find yourself holding onto clutter and old stuff? *Because maybe one day, you will need them.*

Well, have a closer look at your wardrobe. How would you feel about getting rid of your old clothes? How much of old energy is actually accumulating in your personal objects and surroundings? Does the new, 2.0 version of you actually need all this old stuff? Wouldn't it be better to at least do some serious decluttering and release all the old energy while making space for the new?

It's time to have a look at a few timeless Feng Shui tips to make sure you fully affirm your desires while attracting new, empowering energies. Many people worldwide are successfully using these principles to manifest happiness, health, prosperity, and freedom.

The Feng Shui practice focuses on the energy that moves in and around our home and all its rooms. While detailed Feng Shui practices require hiring a professional Feng Shui consultant, the basic principles are easy to understand and apply. They are also very intuitive, some would even say – common sense!

Like in the traditional Chinese medicine, where *chi* is said to flow through the body, in Feng Shui, the *chi*, also called vital force, is thought to flow through our homes.

Clutter is the number one thing you want to get rid of because air and energy elements must always be in motion. And clutter traps all positive energy and keeps us stuck in the past. When I say clutter, I refer to old papers, old books, old clothes, old gadgets, as well as digital clutter, for example, old files on your computer.

Believe it or not, last year, I felt very stuck on my writing journey. So, I decided to declutter my house, paying closer attention to my office and my computer. I immediately felt more energized and creative! I also realized that I was desperately hanging onto some old ideas that originated from my old self and were no longer aligned with my new vision.

I felt scared to get rid of some of my old files because, I thought, maybe one day, I could turn them into bestselling books! I spent a couple of years in this funk. Holding on to several "unfinished manuscripts" that consisted of a few random pages each.

So, whatever it is you're feeling stuck with at the moment, it's time you scheduled some decluttering as soon as possible.

Here are a few more tips:

1.Get rid of all broken items, or have them repaired, replace burned out bulbs, donate, or sell, all things that you have not used in the last 8 months. Let other people enjoy what you're no longer enjoying or aren't passionate about. When you have finished cleaning, wash your hands under running water and sea salt for at least one minute.

2.In Feng Shui, the front door of your house means addressing the issue of the "mouth of chi." So it is essential to help bring good energy into your home by keeping it clean and well lit. You need to remove all the clutter from inside your front door, so you don't block out all the good energy. After you're done with your front door, repeat the process with the other doors in your house as well as your windows.

3. Get ready to use some color therapy in conjunction with decluttering and Feng Shui. You can paint your front door green to attract financial abundance. Red color can bring prosperity and romance. Blue attracts awareness and relaxation. At the same time, brown attracts stability. Even those who don't practice Feng Shui know that experimenting with different colors in your home can drastically change your mood. And by focusing on the activities that put you in a good mood, you automatically manifest more good things into your life.

Plants bring vibrant *chi* into a home or work environment. Home offices require as much good energy as possible, so why not surround ourselves with vibrant and vigorous plants? You can experiment with large plants such as lilies, bamboo, and jade varieties known to be a very high vibe. If you don't have enough space, you can use a smaller plant which is better than nothing. It's essential to keep your plants healthy and well-fed. This can give you a lot of peace and calm. Taking care of your plants is very therapeutic and symbolizes your willingness to invest in yourself and your inner growth.

5.Although most people overlook it, music also plays a significant role in Feng Shui and manifestation. For example, if your home is too quiet, you may create too much *yin* or passive energy. That can affect your mood, making you feel a bit lethargic. So, if you want to manifest higher energy levels, put on some soft music for 10 minutes every day.

6. To attract even more "yang" or good energy, open all your windows when you are cleaning your home. Each room must be ventilated regularly while allowing in some fresh air.

7. Keep all your cleaning equipment in a closet or, if possible, outside your house to block negative energy.

8. A broom even as an ornament for your front door is not recommended since you don't want the positive energy entering your home to be swept away.

9. If your goal is attracting more productivity and creativity, avoid placing your desk in a position directly in front of a window as it can throw all your creativity out. If your goal is to work efficiently, try positioning your desk with the window to one side. So you can look out the window when you need a break without interrupting the flow of creativity.

10. If you want to attract love and romance into your life, have a closer look at your bedroom. Do you sleep in a single or double bed? If you sleep in a double bed, which is your and your partner's side? Are you making space in your home to consciously attract a partner of your dreams? Or does your home scream, "I'm single for life?"

Have a look at your surroundings and start thinking like your new 2.0 version. Create space for new energies and get rid of what is no longer serving you. Mindfully create new habits to keep increasing your quality of life and making your space work for you.

In fact, I highly recommend you start decluttering now! If you're busy, start off with your car, your bag, or your wallet. If your goal is attracting more money and abundance - get a new wallet. Enjoy the feeling of filling it with cash and credit cards!

Also, schedule half an hour of decluttering a day, and start working your way through all your belongings until you're done. If you prefer, you can just go cold turkey and declutter all your belongings in one day.

After getting rid of your clutter and rearranging your space, you will start feeling more peaceful and energized. Help your environment help you! Also, please note, this work never ends. In fact, it should become a habit. I go on regular decluttering sprees several times a year, and it really feels great!

One of the biggest spiritual benefits of decluttering is that you get rid of the resistance of letting go. Old objects you no longer need also represent old mindsets, energies, feelings, and emotions. Ask yourself if you can really afford to hang on to the old? Or are you ready to step up, embrace your new self and finally release whatever it is that's blocking your new levels of manifesting?

Final Words

Keep expanding and keep moving forward!

Remember that you attract who you are. So, keep aligning your thoughts, feelings, and actions with what you want. Watch your energy transform. Embody your desires. Be your desires. Affirm your desires with what you do and how you think about yourself, not only with what you say.

Don't get discouraged or impatient if it takes longer to manifest your desires; the journey itself is your destination. As you are exploring yourself and your manifestation abilities, you are becoming a better person. You are kind to yourself and others while cultivating a positive mindset infused with endless gratitude. That alone is a gift to those around you!

Keep practicing what you have learned, and keep sharing these concepts with others. Together we can change the world by collectively enhancing the vibration of the planet.

I genuinely hope that this book inspired you and gave you new tools to expand your consciousness and raise awareness.

You are limitless, you are powerful, and you are amazing!

I believe in you and wish you all the best on your journey!

Part 2 – Book 2

Script to Manifest

It's Time to Design & Attract Your Dream Life (Even if You Think it's Impossible Now)

By Elena G. Rivers

Copyright Elena G. Rivers © 2020

Introduction

Script to Manifest Your Desires

If you have a wish you'd like to manifest, you've come to the right place. This book will teach you everything you need to know about scripting so that you can start living your life by design.

But, before we dive into it, I want to be 100% honest and transparent with you. Even though scripting is one of my favorite Law of Attraction (LOA) methods, and I practice it every day, it will not work for everyone.

As someone who has been studying, researching, and teaching LOA for years and is particularly fond of the scripting method, I can tell you right here, right now, that it will not work for you in the following cases:

- Case 1 - Scripting will not work if the goal or wish you desire to manifest is not intrinsically yours, or you don't feel any connection with it. For example, you come across some random goal as you think it is expected of you, or because everyone around you is doing it. Perhaps everyone you know is manifesting amazing travels. And so, you think you should travel too because everyone is posting about their globe-trotting adventures on social media. But maybe you're not really into traveling, or you are, but you want to do things your way and visit different places. Whatever the goal is, make sure it's your own!

- Case 2 - The same is also true if you're chasing validation or significance. For example, you want to manifest a Ferrari or Lamborghini because you want other people to give you more respect and call you successful.

Let me explain. There's nothing wrong with desiring nice cars or other "toys" if you're genuinely passionate about them. But ask yourself this: are you a person who can handle and maintain expensive toys without getting freaked out?

Because when you manifest something, you receive the whole package, so you need to understand exactly what you're getting into.

In one of my other books, I shared the story of an acquaintance who manifested a big lottery win in her home country. Unfortunately, she lost it all because she had no idea how to handle large amounts of money; she even got in trouble with her local tax office. The reasons she originally wanted to manifest money were to feel loved and significant. She experienced those emotions fleetingly while having money, but then she lost it all and ended up exactly where she was before winning the lottery. Luckily, she used her experience as an essential life lesson and decided to do the inner work. As a result, she transformed her mindset and energy to become a person who can handle "the whole manifestation package." Now, she's manifesting abundance through her new business. She loves it! She no longer chases validation or approval; instead, she focuses on adding value to the world and providing an excellent service to her clients while manifesting her own money (and being very good at managing it!).

So, just a word of warning here! Are you ready to handle the whole package? Or do you want something purely because it will make you "look better"?

- Case 3 - You want to manifest something out of fear because you don't love yourself. An example of such a mindset is when a person "tries hard" to manifest love and romance, simply because they don't love themselves. They are desperate to find a partner: either to feel loved; or because they fear being single. Unfortunately, such a mindset can lead to negative manifestations. For example, a person can manifest a relationship that is draining or abusive for both parties. A much better and more empowering mindset is when a person already loves themselves and then intends to manifest a dream partner because they love the idea of sharing their life with someone else. They don't need another person to feel loved because they already feel whole and complete. Instead, they desire to manifest a partner from a place of love and with the intention of being in a healthy relationship. They are not desperate while trying to escape the feeling of being alone. So, ask yourself: do you want to manifest because you genuinely love your goals and desires, and you feel good about getting closer to them, or do you want to manifest to escape the pain and you are using your manifestations as a quick "cure"?

- Case 4 - Scripting might not be useful if you don't like writing things down. The scripting method is perfect for "journaling junkies" like me. We love making notes, and we adore having different journals. We actually look forward to our little rituals around writing, planning, expecting, and whatnot. It's fun! I don't know about you, but when I go to bed, I'm already excited for the next morning because I know that I'm going to be enjoying a pleasant morning cup of coffee while doing my little scripting ritual. It's fun for me, so I don't need to "try to stay motivated" or discipline myself to do it.

I always say – different strokes for different folks. You know who you are and what you naturally like or don't like. And since like attracts like and everything happens for a reason, I'm sure that most of the readers I attract are into the same or similar stuff that I'm into.

So, my guess is that you enjoy getting new journals and filling them with your desires.

But I also know that some of you might be getting this book out of curiosity. Or perhaps you are previewing a free sample before getting invested in it, which is a brilliant thing to do.

Once again, don't force yourself into a method just because everyone is doing it. If you're not into journaling, allow yourself to dive into other LOA ritual – have a look at my book catalog and pick something you feel naturally attracted to.

There is one little exception, though. You can learn more about scripting and apply its principles to mindfully formulate your wishes and re-program your subconscious mind while using a different vehicle. For example, a friend of mine learned the scripting method from me, but she's one of those people who don't really like writing things down in their journals. So, what she did instead was, she wrote her vision just once, and then she recorded it. She listens to it while commuting to work, which amounts to a solid hour a day. One of the things she put on her vision was:

"I'm so happy and grateful that my salary is always rising, and I always attract unexpected streams of income; because now I can take care of my family and live a life of fun!".

Within just a few weeks of doing her "audio scripting" while driving to work, she had already manifested a significant salary raise, and one of her side businesses also took off! Now, she's correspondingly manifesting a consistent monthly passive income from her ventures.

- Case 5 - And finally, the most important point I need to make is that scripting will not work if you just use it as a technique without fully understanding the central law of attraction and manifestation principle, which is:

It's not about what you do. It's about who you are and who you become.

And, *it's not about what you want. It's about who you are.*

You manifest what you hold inside.

In other words, it's all about your self-image. For example, you may "try hard" to make more money. You are looking for a new job, business opportunity, or some investments to become a six-figure earner. And yes, from a logical standpoint, it's a pretty smart thing to do. Unfortunately, if you don't already think and feel like a six-figure earner, chances are you will sabotage your efforts. I've seen it time and time again, and I've been there myself; I spent years chasing and chasing.

It was only when I decided to see myself as the person I wanted to become that I actually became that person, and things began to change. So, the first thing you need to do is to decide who you desire to become. Most people fail with manifesting their true desires because they mindlessly "try" to focus on what they want, without ever even attempting to change themselves. It's like trying to alter the reflection in the mirror without changing the person or object standing in front of it. I don't know about you, but I think it's total madness. Although, I don't want to get arrogant and judgmental because I've also been guilty of chasing my "wants" without wondering how to change myself.

As they say, the devil is in the details. It's sad but true. Many people think they already know "all this self-image stuff" because they know who they want to become in terms of status. But, they still do it wrong because they focus more on what they dislike about their old selves and they hardly ever think about their new, empowered selves. In alignment with such a negative mindset, they are still stuck in the past; blaming, judging, and criticizing. They never take any proactive action to upgrade who they are; their feelings, thoughts, behaviors, or skills.

I highly recommend you do this exercise right here and right now by answering the following questions in as much detail as you can (by the way, this is a fantastic pre-scripting preparation exercise!).

It's time to explore your New Self:

- How do you react when things don't go your way?
- Do you choose to complain and feel like a victim?
  Or do you choose to use unfavorable circumstances as valuable life lessons to help grow and improve yourself?
- How do you feel about learning and investing in yourself? What about the people you surround yourself with? Are they into reality creation?
  Do they have goals, ambitions, and desires that they love working towards?
- How do you treat yourself, your body, and your mind?
- How do you talk to yourself?
- Do you choose to focus on your progress? Or are you still stuck in your old ways, feeling guilty about what went wrong?

- How much time do you need to let go?
  5 minutes, 5 days, or 5 years?
- What movies do you play in your mind?
- Do you consciously use your mind to visualize what can go well?
  Or do you choose to play negative movies in your mind?
- How do you fuel your body?
- Do you choose to eat healthy, whole, nutritionally balanced foods?
- How do you feel about investing in your health and wellbeing?
- What do you do when you feel stressed?
  Do you choose to go for a walk, meditate, or watch an inspirational video?
  Or are you stuck inside, feeling bad, scrolling through social media, and drinking or smoking?

We are doing this pre-scripting exercise for a reason. And, as you have probably noticed, for now, we don't focus on things such as what clothes you wear, where you live and what car you drive.

First things first! I see so many people discovering the concept of self-image and jumping into superficial self-image creation such as:

My new self wears designer clothes and lives in a nice neighborhood; my new self is a six-figure earner, and my new self attracts fantastic relationships.

And no, I'm not saying it's bad to want nice clothes and things, but once again, you are focusing on "what," not on "who". You believe you are working on your new self-image, whereas in reality, you still think like your old self, but with nice things around you.

In other words, you want to change the reflection in the mirror without wanting to change the person in front of it. It's all about your mindset, habits, reactions, behaviors, and energy. So before you get into scripting, design a new, powerful self-image with better habits, a more empowered mindset, and new behaviors. It's as simple as that.

Back to my story with scripting...

Yes, I used scripting as my primary manifestation method. However, I was already crystal clear on what made me tick, who I was, and what my authentic desires were. I got rid of all the "inner noise" and superficial goals.

Whatever it is that you do, remember you are sending out signals to the Universe all the time, even when you're not practicing any particular LOA technique or method such as scripting. So be sure to regularly check-in with your mindset and energy.

Let's go back to our previous example. Let's say you desire to manifest a six-figure job. So, how do you feel now when checking your bank account? Empowered? Or ashamed? How do you think and walk? Where do you go on vacations? What charities do you donate to?

A person could have the best scripting method ever and spend hours scripting every day. However, they could also go about their day and do their activities feeling hopeless, therefore negating any positive signals they sent out during their scripting sessions.

No wonder it doesn't work for some people. Or, we could say, it does work because the LOA always works. However, it may not be working in their favor because their mindset and energy are still in a negative vibration.

What we want is full alignment!

You want to stay in check 24/7 and protect your mind and energy from negative influences as much as you can. Yes, use scripting as your secret method to remain focused on the positive. But also, strive to catch any negative habits or patterns you may be still holding onto and promise yourself to mindfully release them.

Don't feel bad about yourself when you experience a negative emotion. It's just a sign for you to let go. It's only feedback from the Universe reminding you to keep releasing your old vibrations while cleansing your mindset and energy.

Scripting will help you stay focused and grounded, and as you go through the techniques shared in this book, you will be raising your vibration. You will feel amazing. Your energy and mindset will shift, and every day, you will love yourself and your reality deeper and deeper, therefore attracting more good things, people, and circumstances into your life!

So now, with this pretty long intro out of the way, let's talk about scripting!

Chapter 1

The Life-Changing Secrets of Scripting Revealed

The main goal of scripting is to support your desire by giving it all your attention, energy, and focus. It makes you get used to your wishes so that they no longer feel far away. In other words, with scripting, you can fuse yourself with your vision instead of putting it on a pedestal. It's also very relaxing and creative because you get to empower yourself with some highly vibrational words.

Unfortunately, in this day and age, most people use a very disempowering language, which, more often than not, keeps them trapped in old, negative energies.

But with scripting, you can choose beautiful, confident, and vibrationally charged words to manifest your desires with joy and ease. Yes, it's all about writing to feel good! It's so much fun because you can formulate your wish list and become a mindful creator of your life.

The primary key to coming up with your wish list is that it must resonate with you. For example, let's say you write:

"I love how I feel knowing that I could easily manifest my dream partner."

Or:

"I love how I feel knowing that I could easily manifest a six-figure job."

"I love how I feel knowing that I could manifest my dream house."

What are the primary emotions you experience?

If you feel excited, expectant, happy, and positive, and you can see yourself as a person who's already living in your dream reality (even if you don't know the *how*), then your wish is truly yours.

The use of the phrase: *"I love how I feel knowing that I could easily manifest ...."* allows you to indicate your desire in a way that makes it real for you. When this happens, you send out a positive vibration to the Universe. In alignment with that, it doesn't matter how often you read or say your wish statement each day.

You want to focus on the quality of your vibration instead, and the best way to do this is to make sure you're working on your true goals, wishes, and desires. In other words, they must come from your heart and soul, and you must be able to see and feel yourself already living your dream!

Your main job is to identify what you want and give it positive attention, energy, and focus, knowing that you are sending out a positive vibration as you do.

Eliminate your doubts and negative vibrations by focusing on what can go well and why you deserve to manifest your desires.

Let's have a look at some examples to help you come up with your own ideas. Remember, it's not about copying other people's scripts word for word. Although yes, you could do that, if it feels right for you. However, you can also use them as inspiration to help you write your own.

Example Scripts:

Sample Script to Attract More Customers/Clients/Contracts:

- I am in the process of attracting and allowing everything I need to do, know and have to attract my ideal client/customer/contract.

This script uses the phrase "I'm in the process." This phrase is recommended for people who tend to give up on their goals because they feel overwhelmed and think their destination is too far away. So, if you create a statement such as, *"I now make 20k a month every month,"* and it feels like a big stretch for you, so because of that, you start doubting yourself, you can soften it up by using the phrase *"I'm in the process."* For example: *"I'm now in the process of raising my income to 20k a month, and I love the person I'm becoming. It's so empowering"*.

More examples:

- *I love how it feels when I attract high-end clients. All my clients are educated, love to invest in themselves, are polite, do the work and pay on time. I love it when they recommend my services to their friends, because like attracts like.*

- *I love the idea of receiving emails or phone calls from my ideal clients, especially when they get great results and want to share them with me. I love how it feels to know that my ideal clients are so impressed with their results that they tell others about my services, thus attracting more ideal clients. I love the idea of working 8-10 hours a week as a coach to my ideal clients. The Law of Attraction is in the process of developing and orchestrating this now. I just love it because it feels so magical!*

Example script to attract more abundance:

- *I am in the process of attracting and allowing everything I need to attract my abundance. I love how it feels when I am gifted free lunch, coffee, or dinner. It always works! I am excited whenever I get free advice, free drinks, free parking, a coupon, a discount, or someone offers to help me for free. I love the idea of getting money from unknown sources. The Law of Attraction is in the process of developing and orchestrating this now. It really feels magical!*

Example script to attract more love:

- I am in the process of attracting and allowing everything I need to attract my ideal love relationship.

- I love the idea of going on walks with my dream partner. I love the idea of packing a lunch and eating at the beach with my love. I love how it feels to know that the conversation is positive, uplifting, and supportive. The Universal Law of Attraction is in the process of developing and orchestrating this now. It feels so magical!

Using Numbers to Manifest Faster

As Pythagoras once said: *"Numbers rule the world."*

And, we can use this to our advantage by leveraging the 3x33 method.

3x33 manifestation is a powerful Law of Attraction writing technique that combines the power of spiritual numbers, intention, focus, emotion, and repetition to fill the subconscious mind with the desire or goal we wish to manifest.

But before I dive into the method itself, I'd like to explain why it works. When you work with the 3x33 method, you activate the energy of number 3; the Divine feminine on the Kabbalistic tree of life. Feminine energy is the energy of life and creation.

So, if you have a series of situations and projects that are scattered or remain unfinished, it's time to use the Divine feminine energy with your scripting rituals. It's all about writing your intentions from a place of love and in a transparent way.

Script to Manifest

The 3x33 method and its variations for busy people

You first choose an intention (something you want to manifest), and then you create a simple statement about that intention.

Then you write out this affirmation 33 times a day for 3 days.

I know, I know. You're probably thinking, "What? 33 times? That's too many!"

And here is where I need to clarify one thing... It's all about quality over quantity... Although yes, the original method indeed tells us that we should write 33 affirmations every day for 3 days, the most important thing is your pure intention.

It's all about being in the present moment while writing your affirmations. You want to think and feel how blessed you are to be receiving. This is why it's absolutely fine to make modifications, such as write your affirmation 3 times for the next 33 days (my favorite idea because it helps you develop mindful consistency and discipline without burning yourself out).

Whatever you choose to do, it's all about mindful repetition; write 33 times for 3 days, 3 times for 33 days, or 9 times for 3 days. Our beliefs are formed in our minds through continuous repetition of that thought over and over again.

Don't forget to use "I am" at the beginning of your affirmations. Since our mind is already accustomed to being addressed with "I am" we will continue this "I am" pattern of internal dialogue in our affirmations as well.

Your affirmations can also include words that express positive emotions such as *happy, grateful, feeling blessed, lucky, etc.*

These are powerful words because they naturally put you in a state of bliss, gratitude, and abundance. Therefore, use them lavishly in your scripted affirmations.

As you probably already know, your affirmations, statements, or scripts (whatever you want to call them) must be written in the present tense. Use a sentence that begins with "I am now...", "I have now...", etc. The idea is to feel grateful; like your wish has already been fulfilled.

Also, don't use the phrase "I want" in your affirmations. By saying, "I want," you automatically imply that you don't have it, therefore sending out a very negative vibration to the Universe. Some unhappy souls get stuck in "wanting" for years, and it only helps them manifest how to be a better "wannabe."

Do You Speak, Think, and Act to Manifest? Or Do You Block Your Manifestations Without Even Knowing?

Your language patterns are fundamental, and there are many words I highly recommend you choose to let go of accordingly.

For example, instead of saying:

"I am trying to,"

say:

"I am playing," or "I am experimenting."

To say that you are trying automatically allows the massive possibility of failure and even a lack of genuine commitment. For example, instead of saying, "I am trying this new business idea," I prefer to say: "I am experimenting with this new opportunity," or "I am learning about it."

You see, when you experiment or learn, there's no space to fail.

When you experiment, you always get a result that will teach you something. There's no such thing as a negative outcome; it's just an outcome, which is some kind of valuable feedback and data.

Instead of saying "I want to," say "I choose to," or "I intend to". Both are much more powerful!

Wanting makes us wannabes. By definition, a wannabe wants something because he or she doesn't have it. If you're a pro at something, you already have it and you do it. It's absolutely normal for you.

As we have already mentioned, you can also say that you're in the process of manifesting something. Expressing that you are "in the process" is an excellent way to help you reduce resistance. This is extremely helpful if you set big goals and massive intentions, and maybe you get a bit nervous. If you state that you're in the process, it'll calm you down; almost on autopilot.

Move on with clarity and be decisive. For example, if you desire to become a business person, focus on one venture until successful. You can't be halfway in and halfway out.

Also, avoid "maybes" and "when I get this, then I'll…" thought patterns. Why not get there directly?

Maybe there's a direct flight.

Alignment is vital since you don't want to be in chaos vibrations or don't want to manifest "maybes" or "I'll do this when…" situations.

How do you know how to make the right decision and script about the right things?

Well, I can't tell you precisely, as I can't make any decisions for you. You see, I used to let other people decide for me, and then whenever I manifested what I didn't want, I'd blame them and not myself. I want to stay away from such energy. Making decisions is also a muscle. Follow your gut!

Be specific, and don't be vague. This is where scripting can help. You can use your script as a tool to help you "taste your new reality;" to see what you like and how you feel. You can also script to stretch your mindset and realize where your weak points are to let them go.

Reverse engineer what worked for you. Think about all the fantastic things you've achieved so far. I'm sure you were specific, that idea just came to your mind, and you knew it was the right thing to do. Reverse engineering what already worked for you is one of the best tools because you and your own life are your best mentors, seriously!

Please note, journaling and scripting can't be done from a place of scarcity. It's not about how much time you spend writing in your journal or what kind of journal you use, just like it's not about how many vision boards you make and how long you visualize for. It's all about your feelings and the emotion behind them. Yes, sometimes you may find yourself feeling like a robot, so be aware of it and focus on something that makes you feel good. Dance, or do some quick yoga pose.

You attract who you are, so if you feel empty, then you'll attract like. Keep your mind and soul open to different sensations.

Some people prefer to record themselves and then listen to their intentions. Audio scripting works for many of my friends, but I prefer traditional scripting and journaling.

Whenever scripting, what I highly recommend is to first be in high vibration or to meditate beforehand.

After you do that, get clear on what you intend to manifest. Then, you can visualize, write, or affirm. Whatever you choose to do, make sure to include lots of positive, expressive words: words that make you feel good and give you an emotional high. Deeply feel the emotions while doing so. Finally, just let it go and move on with your daily activities with good energy.

Using different manifestation methods such as scripting isn't meant to obtain something for you. Manifestation methods are used to tune your vibration to become a vibrational match to your desire.

If you're practicing scripting every day because you're feeling anxious or impatient about your desire, then you'll massively put off your success. So, use scripting to feel good about your desire. I always say it's not so much about what you do, but how you do it.

When I do my gratitude journaling or scripting, I do it because it feels good to me, and I enjoy living in the moment of mindfully putting my desires on paper. Then, I know I'm on a vibrational match to them.

The question I very often get asked is:

So, do I just write about the experiences that I want to have? Because I don't really want anything materialistic. I want to manifest health and happiness. How do I do it the right way?

Answer:

There's really no "wrong" way to journal anything; it's different for everyone. Just make sure you're writing in the present tense - as if you're currently living the life you want and feel the emotions while you do it. Be specific about the happy moments you intend to manifest. For example, "Every weekend, I enjoy amazing parties in beautiful locations. I eat sophisticated dinners with interesting people. I laugh and have fun."

Or: *"Every evening, I hang out with my kids, and we laugh and play."*

Manifesting isn't just about money. Even if a person wants to manifest financial abundance, the subconscious mind finds it *hard to understand the money and numbers; however, it can easily align with the feeling of freedom and happiness.*

At the same time, many of my readers who tried to manifest abundance for years (yeah, they tried, and nothing happened) suddenly began manifesting unexpected income just by focusing on manifesting happiness first.

Some food for thought!

I can personally attest to the holistic effectiveness of focusing on manifesting happiness and peace of mind. The rest becomes easier, and all the resistance gets removed.

Be very mindful of your language. Use words that empower and send out the vibration of conviction and confidence, not lack or unworthiness.

The affirmation should convey that the desire is here and is already part of our reality.

Also, remember to have fun with your desires, but don't get too obsessed. Ask yourself, if you already had your desires, how would you feel about them? Would you feel stressed that it's "taking too long"? Of course not. Because it would feel normal to you.

This is where the Normalization Method comes in. It's as simple as affirming: *It's normal for me to...*

Example: *It's normal for me to attract high-quality clients.*

It's normal for me to travel the world while doing what I love for a living.

It's normal for me to work my dream job!

It's normal for me to feel amazing in my body.

It's normal for me to have a six-figure business.

It's normal for me to feel healthy and energized. In fact, every day, I feel better and better. I thrive.

It's normal for me to enjoy vibrant health!

It's normal for me to attract kind and loving people into my life.

The Hidden Dangers of Not Letting Go

You also need to master the art of letting go. Once again, no complicated rituals are required. For our scripting purposes, letting go means mindfully addressing any doubts, worries, or anxiety associated with our intention.

For example, let's say you keep writing, "I'm so grateful I'm now making a steady six-figures in my job/business. I love the people I work with; it's so much fun!".

And then you suddenly start experiencing a negative emotion, thinking:

"OMG, but what if I make more money and I begin to lose my friends? What if they start feeling jealous or feel bad?"

Many LOA teachers would tell you to dismiss it as some negative thought and just keep writing or reciting: *"Oh, but I'm a six-figure earner, and I'm so happy"* (but this can inadvertently create resistance and, more often than not, leads to you manifesting what you don't want, or sabotaging your efforts). However, we want to use any negative thoughts that come up as clues and valuable feedback.

So, take a break from writing or affirming, and ask yourself:

- *How would the new 2.0 version of myself think? Would I really feel that way?*

As a result, you may start coming up with different answers, therefore reducing resistance:

- Well, I will find out who my real friends are. My real friends will be inspired, not jealous! And if they are motivated, then they too can reach more success if they want to.

- Life is not only about money. If some of my old friends are not into increasing their salaries and incomes, that's fine. We can still enjoy each other's company and talk about other passions and interests that we share.

- If I make more money, then I will be able to help those around me. I can already feel this great peace of mind that money can offer. I'm a good person, and money will amplify it. I can only feel good about myself because I'm an ambitious person, and I deserve a well-paying job or business.

Or perhaps as you go writing your vision, you start worrying:

- Hmm...but if I make more money, my taxes will be more complicated. Is it really worth it?

And then, once again, explore that inner resistance. How would your 2.0 version think? Would they worry about it? Of course not. So, you can start soothing your subconscious mind by affirming:

- I can trust myself with making more money and doing my taxes. I always attract great people into my life. Now, I'm in the

process of attracting a tax expert who can help me. It is a win-win! It's safe for me to make more money.

Maybe you will even feel inspired to book a consultation with a financial planner or a tax expert, acting exactly as if you were already making your desired income. If not, why not?

I used this exact same method to manifest my ideal weight without any restrictive dieting, just eating a whole food diet, most of the time. I remember writing down my affirmations while experiencing an incredible resistance, such as:

Oh, but if I lose weight, then my sister and family members will feel jealous. I mean, she used to be a ballet queen as a teen, and now she's put on weight. If I lose weight, she will feel bad, and so will my mom.

So, I began to explore that thought because I wanted to empower it and turn it into something positive. I visualized myself at my ideal weight. I saw my family telling me how great I looked and that they too feel inspired to lose weight, asking if I wanted to help them.

I began writing down a new affirmation:

I am so grateful for my ideal weight, healthy lifestyle, and incredible energy levels. I'm even more thankful that my loved ones could join me on this journey and reach their health and weight loss goals with me. Now, we go hiking together. We go to healthy organic restaurants together. We mindfully change our habits together, and it's so much fun!

It worked very well for all of us! Which proves the importance of exploring our negative thoughts and resistance. No, we don't dwell on the negative. We use it to transform our lives and manifest our dream reality with joy and ease, for the highest good of all involved.

Also, please note that some people are just not ready to change. Yes, they may judge you; they may criticize you because you decided to shine and live life on your own terms. But don't allow their negative vibration to destroy your dreams. Don't be a people pleaser. Choose to raise up and live to your new standards. Those who get inspired will reach out for help, and those who get jealous only harm themselves, not you.

So, never feel inadequate for formulating new desires and affirmations aligned with your unique vision for life. Stop asking for approval and concerning yourself with what other people think of you.

Focus on the fact that there are numerous techniques to reinforce the reality you long for. One of the most powerful is the written word, and you are already using it to mindfully create your own reality!

The Ivory Tower Scripting Trap to Avoid!

Sometimes you may find yourself creating an affirmation that eventually stops being fun or loses its meaning. It no longer feels right for you because your goals have shifted. Then, you may find yourself feeling stuck.

Remember, this is just feedback. Any negativity you experience in your mind can be transformed into a new, positive vision. You can always change direction!

To do this, you must create a vision for your desired life that is as detailed as possible. Write about it in your journal. Design your perfect life, your expected life. Besides writing about it, allow yourself to live it as much as you can, right here and right now.

I keep a daily diary of my desired life. I use it to capture a life in which I already have everything I want, and consequently, the Universe does not hesitate to follow my clear instructions.

Below are the three journaling tips you absolutely can't miss:

1.- Be super detailed and follow your intuition

For example, if you want to attract a perfect house, you can write:

"I am grateful to wake up every day in my wide and comfortable bed from which I can see the sea and the sky through the terrace window. The sheets are blue, soft, and

smooth. I can hear the seagulls and the sound of the waves breaking in the distance. I love the smell of the sea. I drink coconut latte on my terrace while planning my day. My partner calls me for breakfast. We're going to enjoy some delicious homemade pancakes and marmalade."

When writing, use all your senses: see, hear, touch, smell and taste your new reality.

By writing things down in detail, you will also find it much easier to visualize your desires.

The first step is always to capture what you want, not what you don't want. Always write in the present and in the first person. Mentally screenshot the best and most exciting parts of your dream so that you can later use them in your visualizations. This can be a terrific complementary method.

Many people fail with this exercise because they write in the future tense while just "hoping" for something to manifest. And tomorrow never comes. Instead, you want to write with conviction and unleash the power of the present moment.

Remember, the Universe doesn't like to feel confused. So, express yourself clearly, say what you want, and supercharge it by feeling good. You deserve it, and you have it.

Accompany your writing with photos and drawings that reinforce your vision. For example, you can use pictures of a beach sunrise, an elegant bedroom, and a superior interior design.

Use your favorite colors to highlight the most relevant words you write. Colors can elevate your vision and make it vibrate at a higher level.

2.- Your scripting ritual should be a blessing, not an obligation.

This is very important. Never write out of obligation, do it only if you want to. Also, don't think that by writing more, you will attract your dreams faster.

In nature, everything needs time. For example, it takes nine months to give birth to a baby. It's not that with nine women, it will take only a month.

The most important thing is the vibration you emit when you write. You are really living what you describe in your journal.

If one day you don't feel like writing or can't focus on it for whatever reason, that's fine. You can re-read what you have already written or simply rest... Tomorrow is another day, and you will feel refreshed. This is not a competition, and you have nothing to prove. Enjoy writing or don't write!

If you don't have time for writing, ask yourself, *What can I do to read or feel my vision every day?*

- Perhaps I can take a picture of my writings and keep it on my phone. Whenever I feel tempted to mindlessly scroll on social media, I can scroll on my vision instead.

- Perhaps I can record my vision and listen to it in my car on my commute to work.

There's always a plan B. There's still something to fall back on!

3.- Support your writing with action.

Do whatever you can do to keep moving forward. Take inspired action. Start acting "as if." If you're in the process of manifesting a significant salary raise, talk to a financial planner or accountant who has experience working with wealthy people.

If you are in the process of manifesting a healthy body, start going to healthy food stores, or book a holistic cooking class. Invest in a professional consultation with a naturopath or nutritionist. Instead of watching TV, go for a walk.

If you desire to be well-known for your work; you want to be the number-one-to-go-to expert, perhaps your next bold step would involve enrolling in some professional course. Or maybe you could talk to a marketing expert to learn how to put yourself out there, get leverage and get your work known by more people.

If you are an entrepreneur who is now scaling your business, well, perhaps the next step will be to change your business structure. Maybe you are too big now to do your business as a sole proprietor. Perhaps it's time to upgrade and register as a company or a corporation. How about hiring employees? The next step would be to talk to an expert and get familiar with a new plan.

Yes, it will feel very uncomfortable at first. Your mind will tell you, *"Oh, but I'm not there yet. I can't do this. Maybe, I need to wait."*

But guess what, it's all about Calculated Vibration Raises! Yes, you also need to stretch yourself and show the Universe that you are committed. You already are the person who can handle the Whole Manifestation Package. You can handle growth; you can handle talking to financial experts; you can handle eating a healthy diet; you can handle joining the gym. You can handle whatever it is that the new, 2.0 version of you is already doing with your eyes closed, pretty much automatically.

So, if it's a house you want, you can visit it. Arrange a visit with a real estate agent. Enjoy the process of touring your dream house and feel the energy; imagine yourself living in it. Now it will be much easier for you to write about it. You can even declare, "This is my house."

You can't fail: you either succeed, or you learn. You can only get closer to your goals.

It's like a little kid who gets new shoes that turn out to be a bit too big. Eventually, he or she will grow into them. So, don't be afraid. Your time will come!

The best part is that you will be someone who can handle them when you manifest your desires. You will not sabotage your success by reverting back to your old self, old feelings, thoughts, and actions that no longer resonate with your new goals.

Unfortunately, most people miss that part. They want to write about their desires, but they never take any aligned action. Sometimes, they may manifest what they want, but since they are not used to the Full Manifestation Package, they can't handle their achievements. For example, a person can manifest a rise in their income. But, because they never prepared for it and never talked to a professional financial planner or high-level accountant, they may mismanage their money.

Don't be that person; be a smart manifestor. Prepare yourself, do your research, talk to experts. Learn and grow. Leave your comfort zone.

Remember, if the goals you desire to manifest are indeed yours, it means that your 2.0 version already knows how to handle the Full Manifestation Package. You want to fuse yourself with your new version by gradually changing your feelings, thoughts, actions, and habits.

Things that used to irritate you don't bother you anymore. Your old problems no longer exist. If anything, you get new "problems," which are better quality problems.

Example – Old self: *It's hard to pay the bills!*

New Self: *Money is no longer a problem. In fact, I can start investing. My new quality "problem" is that I need to find a good investment expert to learn from.*

You want a new car? Visit the dealership. If it's a new job, try visiting their offices. Talk to people who work there. Maybe there is a way to do business with them now?

Seeing your desire in reality will motivate you and help you to persevere.

Today is the perfect day to start with this diary of your desired life. What do you want? What is your dream? Capture it with your mindful scripting rituals.

Remember that the Universe will always give you what you feel you deserve. Feel good, and you will attract good.

Chapter 2

LOA for Skeptics (Why It Will Work for You If You Choose So!)

Have you ever wondered why, after hearing about a specific book, concept, word, term, or number, you suddenly start seeing it everywhere? Perhaps you've joined some spiritual communities where everyone is talking about seeing repetitive numbers such as 11:11 or 22:22. And now, you too can see repetitive numbers all around you, and become to feel intrigued! Is it magic? Or something else? Personally, I think it's magic because we are magical, and so are our brains! But there's also a scientific explanation behind it.

You see what you choose to focus on. You see repetitive numbers because of the big bundle of nerves sitting at the end of your brainstem: the Reticular Activating System (RAS).

The RAS is what makes the Law of Attraction work. And it always works. It's totally up to you to choose to wake up and begin to consciously program yourself, scripting your life in the way you desire.

Script to Manifest

Your RAS registers what you focus on and creates filters to display what's on your mind. In other words, it uses its smart algorithms to show you precisely what it thinks you most desire to see.

There is a little problem though! While the RAS is good at showing you what it thinks you want to see or what drives your attention, it isn't great at understanding what you truly want.

It can only determine what you focus on - that's it. So ask yourself, what's on your mind? What do you feed it with? Do you focus on what you desire?

For example, if your desire is to buy a beautiful home, but you keep focusing on how impossible it is to get a mortgage and that everything is so expensive while salaries are going down, well, guess what your RAS is going to do?

It will quickly figure out, "OK, you are looking for more proof and evidence to see how impossible or even dangerous it is to buy your own house. Let's do this. Your wish is my command!"

Simultaneously focus on what you want by using scripting, good feelings, and visualizations. Your RAS will do everything it can to make you more aware of fantastic house opportunities waiting for you.

The amount of effort it takes is pretty much the same once you understand the importance of positive focus.

Although yes, to be absolutely honest with you, it may feel a bit draining when you first get started. It's like going to a Spirituality Gym and building up your Positive Focus Muscle while making RAS work in alignment with your desires.

So, what do you choose?

Choosing to ignore your RAS is especially dangerous in today's social media world, where it's easy to fall into false information that reinforces what you already believe, not necessarily what's right or in alignment with what you want.

This is the reason why I deleted most of my social media profiles and stopped scrolling. Instead, I concentrated on doing inner work while mindfully working on my focus. As a result of my work, my RAS began presenting me with positive filters that would lead me to my goals.

This is the real science behind the Law of Attraction. What you focus on expands, and it eventually becomes your reality. It happens pretty much on autopilot, and yet most people never wake up. They never even attempt to re-program their inner filters while changing their existence. It's a question of choice.

So, why do I mention all this? Well, perhaps as you're reading this book, you're starting to feel doubtful and thinking, *will this work for me?*
But whether you choose positivity or negativity, the fact remains: What you think about, you bring about.

To mindfully create your dream reality, the first step is to see it in your current one.

When you look at the world through a positive, creative lens, opportunities to attract more positivity just pop-up, and it feels like magic!

You can train your RAS and use it to deliver inspiration and the next steps to follow right to your doorstep. Also, remember, positivity isn't just about smiling or pretending to be positive so that everyone around you says: "Oh wow, you are so spiritual and positive."

Real positivity is about being able to step up and solve problems in a creative and empowering way. Genuine positivity is when you are resilient and know how to persevere. So, choose to see the light because there is always light at the end of the tunnel. You are that light!

Chapter 3

Why You Can't Afford Not to Protect Your Dreams!

When you decide to shine your light while emitting more and more positive energy, creating personal and professional success, some negative individuals may attempt to belittle you or make you believe that it's not safe for you to grow.

Remember to stay focused on your journey, no matter what. Different people make different choices, and some people just choose to stay where they are.

Be very mindful of:

- who you surround yourself with

- what you share and with who

- your authentic desires - after all, you want to focus on what you want!

The best way to "deal with negativity" is to allow yourself to get out of it by focusing on positive thoughts, actions, and feelings.

For example, as I began to grow as an author, I quickly noticed that some people who I thought were my "friends" began to gossip or even make jokes about it. I had two choices: go back to where I was before: negative, sad, broke, and taking part in their "drama," or keep raising my vibration; learning, growing, investing in myself, and allowing new people into my life.

I don't know about you, but I have already wasted lots of time in my life, just trying to please others or make them like me.

I would even say I was addicted to "what they will think of me?" at some stage. Well, I had to let it go. I had to carry on doing the inner work while becoming a new person. Now, I'm no longer attracted to drama, gossip, or negativity. I refuse to take any part in it. No, thank you very much.

And this is the best tip I could ever give you: fill your day with as many positive activities as you can and make your inner work a priority. Accept that, as you continue on your Law of Attraction and scripting journey, you will be outgrowing some friends. But, here's one awesome thing to understand; at the same time, you will also be growing into new people, circumstances, and possibilities!

There is an exercise that I learned from Neuro-Linguistic Programing (NLP), and it's very effective in minimizing the effect that the influence of negative people can have on you - primarily, when it affects you explicitly. This exercise consists of redefining the frame of reference with which you see a negative person. You can do it in several ways, and it's lots of fun!

You can visualize that person with a clown nose. This way, every time they say something rude to you, imagine them with a giant clown nose and clown shoes. You can even paint their face if you want to. What they say now comes out of a clown's mouth, so there's no way it can adversely affect you!

You can also imagine that this negative person speaks to you from a tiny box, so you can hardly hear their words. You cannot understand what they say very well because they are in the box! They are so small, and their voice is so low. Therefore, what they say simply doesn't affect you.

You can design any other exercise of this kind that serves to redefine the frame. You are the one who dominates, and you are in an advantageous situation. By doing this, you put yourself in a position of strength that allows you to emit very high and positive vibrations. You create a kind of magnetic field around you, a powerful one that prevents the passage of bad energies while raising your self-esteem.

Remember, don't let other people divert you from your path. You are now scripting your dream reality, and it's in the process of manifesting. This is why protecting yourself and your energy is so important!

Now you understand the primary and most potent principles of scripting. You also know why your focus is essential and how to protect it from negative people and circumstances.

The following pages will give you more inspiration and empowerment to help you mindfully design your life with scripting.

Chapter 4

The Secrets to True Empowerment with Scripting

It's all about creating your own way of scripting. Use the fundamental principles outlined in this book as a template to start working with the Universal Laws. But also be mindful of doing things your way, and feel good about it!

Keep in mind that you need to allow yourself to have a whole life of success. There's no reason to limit yourself. You are not writing a to-do list while desperately trying to think: "*Oh, but will I have time for this today?*"

Instead, you are writing a book of your life, a life well-lived, a life you can be proud of. One of the best ways to do this is to write your scripts as if they were gratitude letters. This technique will help you align with total solutions and endless positive possibilities to help you design a wonderful life.

For example, I used to worry about finances. It was several years ago when I was in debt. Back then, I didn't know much about scripting.

Out of nowhere, I got inspired to write a gratitude letter to the Universe because I wanted to feel better about my situation. I already knew good feelings could help me manifest better things, and writing a gratitude letter seemed like an excellent idea.

So, I took a piece of paper (I wasn't a journaling junkie back then), and I wrote:

It feels so good to have all the money I need to pay my bills, live an extraordinary life, and save up. I'm glad that I finally found a way to get out of debt forever, and now, when I think about it, it seems like some past life.

Money flows abundantly. I don't need to worry about it. All I focus on is doing my passion for a living and helping other people.

I love what I do, and what I do loves me. I get rewarded for my work. Also, I love that I now finally have more time for self-care and can indulge in long walks on the beach. I live on a small island, where it's so peaceful and quiet; people are nice and friendly. I love this place.

Right now, as I'm writing this, I'm chilling on the beach, writing my gratitude letter thinking how far I've come. Thank You, Universe, for allowing me to live my best life.

After finishing my gratitude letter, I saved it in an old cookbook. A few years later, I found it as I was moving houses. And do you know the best part? Not only was I moving houses, but I was also re-locating to a small island in the Atlantic (Fuerteventura,

Canary Islands), and it was exactly what I had written down in my gratitude letter.

Back then, I had no idea how it would happen. The vision literally came out of my subconscious mind as I allowed myself to be in a relaxed, positive state while letting in new energies and infinite possibilities. My vision made complete sense to me. I simply affirmed what I desired and sent out a clear signal to the Universe.

People always ask me what kind of goal to keep in mind while scripting. For example, *should you start small, just to test it and see if it works?*

My answer is, it depends on your mindset and energy.

After years of practicing the LOA, I realized that, for me, setting big goals works amazingly well because they open my mind up to new possibilities. But you must believe it's right for you and the goal must genuinely be yours. Otherwise, you will give up on it, saying, *oh, it's taking too long, it's not working.*

At the same time, many people start off with small goals because they feel insecure about themselves. And it's because of that negative energy that they don't manifest even a tiny dream. They are still thinking: *I guess I should keep shrinking my dreams, and maybe that way I can manifest something.*

So, first things first - get your mindset right, realize who you are and what you truly desire. Then, get your energy right and ask yourself: *Am I attempting to manifest from the energy of lack or abundance? Do I believe in myself? Do I realize that the creative power of the Universe is there to help me?*

Both small and high goal setting can be done successfully if you spend some time adjusting your mindset and energy by answering the above questions.

You can also do both. Set a big goal and treat it as your vision. Then, think of a small goal that serves as a milestone leading you to the bigger one (this is my favorite way of doing things). As you manifest your desires, don't forget to keep expressing your gratitude for all the milestones you've already reached and everything you learned on your journey.

Such an attitude will automatically help you get rid of guilt, shame, or hopelessness that you may experience if you focus too much on your mistakes.

For example, a professional woman is feeling stuck in her job. Her big goal is to be working for herself as a coach in her chosen field, making 10k a month.

Right now, it all seems so far away because in her current job, she's making 5k a month, and she doesn't even like what she does.

But, she still writes a gratitude letter to the Universe. She focuses on every detail in her vision:

Wow, I can't believe it. Today I finally gave my notice and will be leaving my job soon. What used to be my dream and my little side hustle is now making me 10k a month, and I love the work I do. I attract amazing clients who are ready to transform. They follow my programs and get fantastic results. Every day, I get an email or a message from a happy client telling me they recommended my work to their family and friends. The clients just keep coming, and they are all high-end clients. The best part? I work much less than in my current job. In fact, I work only 4-5 hours a day, four days a week. I finally have more time for self-care and self-development, which allows me to develop innovative solutions and better programs for my clients. I'm getting better and better at marketing too! In fact, other coaches are reaching out to me, offering me money to help them market their services. I've never experienced so much abundance in my life! Thank You, Thank You, Thank You!

After specifying her vision and getting very excited about it while already feeling grateful for it, she sets her first milestone: *I'm now making 1k a month or more from my side business as a coach.*

She aligns her actions, thoughts, and feelings with this milestone. She decides to *be* that milestone and truly live it. After all, it doesn't seem like something difficult; she can do it. So, she takes aligned and inspired action from a place of curiosity: *I wonder how it would feel to have that extra 1k a month in my pocket? What would I do with that money? I could easily save to go on a nice vacation, or I could begin to invest in myself and my coaching education. Or I could buy a nice camera and some equipment to start doing YouTube videos and attracting my dream clients.*

Even though she still doesn't have a nice camera or lightning, she already feels unstoppable. She swaps excuses for mindful action. She takes her smartphone and makes inspirational videos to upload to YouTube. In fact, every morning, while driving to work, she records an uplifting video, sharing her knowledge. At the end of each video, she offers personalized, 1:1 help. She's honest, open, and transparent; not afraid to share her personal struggles from a place of authenticity.

After a few weeks, she can easily manifest an extra 1k a month while still working in her job.

Wow, this is working! So, now let's start a new milestone. What about 3k a month?

Instead of looking for excuses, she looks for the evidence that it's already working for her and she can do it. She keeps stretching herself and her vibration in alignment with her new goals. She sees obstacles and challenges as lessons to learn and grow from.

Eventually, her vision becomes her reality, and she manifests a successful, 6-figure career doing what she loves for a living.

Nothing can beat scripting, supercharged with the power of goal setting.

Please remember that you can use this methodology to improve all areas of your life! But, since most people that reach out to me desire to manifest more money, many of the examples of this book focus on money and numbers. Numbers don't lie – they can only tell us if we reach our goals or not. Remember, though, you can use scripting magnified with goal setting to enrich all areas of your life. This brings us to the next question.

People always ask me if it's possible to manifest multiple things at once. My answer is, it's up to you. If you think it's possible for you and you fully believe it, go for it.

Personally, I like to focus on one or two areas of my life at a time. It's because I understand that when you address the areas of life that need most of your attention, other things you desire may manifest automatically. I'm also a big believer in the power of focus.

When I first got started on my scripting journey, my main focus was on my writing and health. And as I began taking mindful action, transforming and manifesting my desires, other areas of my life such as relationships, finance, travel, and spirituality changed as well.

So, ask yourself, which area of your life requires most of your attention now? And which one is next?

For example, if you struggle with low energy and can't lose weight, perhaps you could start with your health. Write out your vision in detail and set your first milestone. Rinse and repeat. Remember to keep taking aligned action and start acting "as if." Allow yourself to move your body; go for lovely, rejuvenating walks instead of watching TV; and swap candy bars for fresh smoothies.

Book a consultation with a nutritionist or naturopath. Yes, the Universe will help by arranging many things for you, but you must keep taking aligned action, showing your commitment, and fusing yourself with your vision by gradually becoming a person who lives that vision. Treat your body like a temple, and other areas of your life will improve as well.

It's all about tapping into the thought process and vibration of what you desire and acting precisely as the 2.0 version of you would!

To sum up:

Step #1 - Start off by writing a letter to the Universe (or whomever you choose to see and identify as the source. You can even write a letter to your higher self, God, your angels; it's really up to you). Be and feel thankful in advance for all your desires coming true.

Step #2 - Fuse yourself with your vision every day. You can read your letter or start writing about different elements of it in your journal. You can also record it and listen to it in your car. If you are really busy, you could even mentally screenshot your gratitude letter and carry it in your mind and heart.

The method I'm using now is that I combine this with my daily gratitude. Every day, I write down several things I'm grateful for, and then I intuitively start adding some elements from my vision, as if they already happened. It makes it so real for my inner mind! Also, I get excited writing about things I'm grateful for (already manifested in my reality), which makes me very confident in my manifestation powers. Then, I add something from my vision and can't help but feel gratitude for it.

Step #3 - If you are still looking for the "right way" to do this, remember that you are the right way. Just focus on really feeling your desires, and evoke emotion.

Step #4 Don't get too obsessed with your vision, torturing yourself with thoughts such as, *"Oh, when will it happen?"*.

Just move on with your life and do your daily activities with joy. Know that something in you has already changed, and your external reality is changing too. Train your mind to start looking for positive proof and evidence of everything working out for you.

Step #5 - For some people, scripting can become robotic. If it does, take a break. Don't force it. The most important thing is to feel the emotion of your desire.

Step #6 - Enjoy it, and Happy Manifesting!

Chapter 5

Your Questions Answered

This chapter is designed to take your scripting journey to the next level by answering the most common questions that people have.

It will help you stay motivated and inspired to manifest faster!

Question: Does it matter what you write your vision on?

Do I need a special journal or paper?

Answer: No. The Universe doesn't think, "you wrote in red ink, and on blue paper, so I'm not listening to you." Instead, it responds to how you feel about what you do. So, choose whatever works for you. If you get excited about your new journal and its beautiful paper, go for it.

If you like your old notebook, use it. And choose whatever color you want. Personally, I love red ink because it makes me feel in control. It makes me feel like the master of my own reality: someone who gets to correct what is out of alignment!

Question: Which one is better? Basic scripts or abundant stories?

Answer: I would suggest abundant stories with as much detail as possible. However, if you're feeling resistance, or can't come up with too much detail, don't worry for now. Start off with a basic script (it can even be one sentence) and go from there. As you begin to re-write your brain and focus on what you actually want while believing that you too can manifest your wildest dreams, your basic scripts will turn into great stories filled with positive emotions, and your reality will start to reflect this. Again, don't force it; let it come.

But also, be persistent and don't give up. Some people find it hard to come up with their vision. There's nothing to worry about, though. Keep exploring different scenarios and possibilities in your mind and start writing them down. This can be a tremendous pre-scripting exercise. When you're ready, come up with your real, authentic vision!

Sometimes you feel like you want so many things but are not too sure which one to pick. Well, writing things down will help you get clarity. Some people feel scared thinking: *"OMG, if I write it down or think about it, it will become my reality."* This is not the case, though! You are just writing different options, and you intend to pick and choose the ones you like.

Also, remember, it's not about perfection, it's about progress. Getting clarity on what you want is hard for many people, and I have been there too. I remember when I first got introduced to the "design your ideal day exercise." It was actually during some business and marketing training, and I felt perplexed. I remember thinking, why don't they just show me how to grow a business and make more money? If they give me the best marketing strategy, then I will surely design a super great life.

What I didn't realize back then is that I was putting the cart before the horse. And well, when it comes to "marketing," manifestation is also like marketing. We market ourselves and our desires to the Universe. So, once again, we need clarity as to which desires we wish to market!

Remember when you were a kid? You had clarity. You knew what you wanted. You didn't hesitate when saying, "I guess this is not for me."

Well, you want to be that little kid, writing their wish list to Santa Claus (or whoever brings presents in your country/culture).

It's all a process, and your real vision will come. Start writing things down to get clarity. There's no way around it.

Question: Is there step-by-step guidance to help me write a detailed vision for all areas of my life?

Answer: Yes. To do it, focus on finance, health, personal relationships, professional relationships, lifestyle (your home, car, vacations), and physical appearance. Some people also like to add spiritual experiences, fulfillment, specific work, passions, etc.

Focus on what matters for you and your vision. For example, if you are an introvert and don't really like having a social life or attending big gatherings, there is no point in adding, "I go out and socialize every day" to your vision just for the sake of it. Unless, of course, you want to manifest becoming a social, extroverted person because it is your real goal.

It all goes back to what we covered in the introduction of this book; focus on goals that are genuinely yours. It's tempting to copy other people's visions, thinking, *"If they are doing well, they are successful, so I'm just gonna do the same."*

This is a big no-no. Tune in with your heart. It knows! Unleash the Power of Self-Coaching, and you can be your primary source of information and inspiration.

Most people keep jumping to the past instead of jumping to their future. The best book you can ever read is your own journal because it is where you write your life, and this is what will get you results.

Below are some self-coaching questions to help you get even more clarity:

-What would you do if you knew you couldn't fail?

-How would that affect you and your recent decisions?

Question: I'm still a bit scared to get started. What if I do it the wrong way and don't manifest anything?

Answer: The only wrong way is when you overcomplicate it or do it as an obligation. You design your own rules! You are in control, and you are empowered to make decisions for yourself.

You are not in school anymore, and I'm not your teacher telling you to write an essay, in a specific style, with 3k words; no more, no less.

I am happy to be your guide and inspire you to get started to be self-sufficient and empowered. It's all about getting started, no matter what you do.

You seem to be stuck in a place of doubt (no judgment here; I have been there as well). Ask yourself: how would it feel to get unstuck by just getting started?

You have nothing to lose, but a lot to gain. This is what self-development is all about, and it should be fun.

You can also use the following steps:

Step#1 - Speak as though your wish had already come true.

Example: "*I am so happy and grateful now that...*

Step#2 - Start expressing your desires daily as though you are experiencing them in your now.

Example: "*I feel so grateful I feel so much energy every single day.*"

"*I'm getting more and more inspired, and my creativity is so abundant!*"

"I feel so grateful that all of my relationships are positive and uplifting!"

Step#3 - Look for love and positivity wherever you are. Always be thankful, and look for more and more things to be grateful for. Trust the Universe because it knows what's right for you and your long-term wellbeing.

Example: *"I'm so grateful to the Universe for allowing all of my dreams into my reality. I love the person I'm becoming. It feels so good."*

- *"I'm grateful that all these amazing opportunities align because the Universe cares for me."*

- *"I know that I'm not alone and that the Universe is always working to create more happiness for me."*

Step#4 - Show your commitment and dedication by taking inspired action in alignment with your vision. Use the following affirmations, or use them as a guide to creating your own that feel good for you:

- *"I'm so grateful for the opportunities I've been given, and I commit to being a vehicle of creativity."*

- *"I radiate my unique, authentic expression to the fullest of my capacity."*

- *"I express myself through my work, for the highest good of everyone involved."*

- *"I commit to being in alignment with my higher self. I share only good thoughts, actions, and feelings with those around me."*

- *"I commit to practicing powerful self-talk. I talk to myself kindly to unleash my full potential."*

Question: Do we have to re-write our script every day? Can we "copy" each day what we previously wrote?

Answer: First of all, get rid of "have to" and "should." Use the word "choose" instead. It's so much more empowering! So, yes, it's up to you. You can choose to re-write your vision if you want to, and you can also rephrase it or focus on some elements of it. It's up to you what you do. But the primary purpose behind it is to fuse yourself with your vision and use scripting methods as a tool.

Question: Can I script and write other things I experience in my life in my regular diary or journal at the same time? Will the Universe get confused on which is my actual scripting?

Answer: The Universe won't get confused unless you feel confused, so it's really up to you. If you want to have two different journals and it feels right for you, go for it. You can organize yourself in the way that best suits you.

Some people like to have just one journal, and they write their daily gratitude intertwined with their scripts. Some want to keep a diary to track what's going on in their head while using a different journal for scripting purposes.

The real question is: what feels right and sustainable for you?

Question:

I want to use scripting to manifest success faster. My dream is to be a businessman. I want to create a high income for myself and those who work for me. I want to build a big company. The problem is that I'm only 17. Do you think it's too early to start?

Answer: Don't ask other people or me for permission or approval. It's clear that you know what you want, and you used powerful, confident language. You also have your why, which is excellent. I think it's wonderful that you have such a big vision at such a young age and want to help other people by creating well-paying jobs for them.

However, you are also quick to negate your vision with a "but." Age is just a number, and you limit yourself by saying what you've said. Yes, legally, in most, if not all countries, you probably can't open a company at your age. But so what? You can still work on your vision and script. You can open your dream company in your mind.

At the same time, you can start taking aligned action by learning more about business. You can enjoy the journey and allow it to lead you to your destination. The mind and what you can achieve in life are limitless if you believe in yourself.

Question: Shall I script in my native language or in English?

Answer: Both are fine. While most people would feel more confident scripting in their mother tongue, there are some exceptions. For example, let's say your native language is French. However, you are also fluent in English, and you are used to reading and studying self-development books in English. In this case, your mind started learning these new concepts in your second language, which is English, and it makes some sense to stick to it in your scripting rituals. But, once again, do what feels right for you. You could even mix two languages if you want. The Universe will respond to your feelings and emotions, so feel free to write in whatever language you want.

Question: I usually write ten things I feel grateful for, and then I write my affirmations every day. Am I doing it right? Are "positive affirmations" and "scripting" the same things or different from each other?

Answer: If you feel good about what you do; use positive, empowering language; write your affirmations in the present tense, and are open to taking inspired action; there's no doubt something beautiful will come out of your endeavors. So, to answer your question, don't worry, you are doing it right. Now, when it comes to comparing scripting to affirmations, there is a little difference:

Affirmation is about writing positive statements.

For example, *Every day, I feel more and more energized.*

Scripting is writing your desires in a story format.

For example, *I wake up in my beautiful beach house. I can hear and smell the ocean. I get up, and I can see my beautiful blue carpet. I just got my Pedi done yesterday, and the nail polish matches my carpet. I go downstairs, drink water, and make myself a nice, nutritious smoothie. It's now 8 o'clock. My yoga teacher is coming at 9, so I'm going to have a quick shower now and then meditate a bit on my terrace. I feel so energized and healthy. It makes me feel excited about my day because I know that many amazing things are coming my way!*

The critical element here is to 'feel the emotions' while we write our desires. So, if you'd like to enhance your journaling practice, be sure to use more feelings in your writing. You can also write your vision in detail using dynamic scripting, then record it and listen to it every day. Pick whatever feels right for you.

Question: Can this be done on my phone instead of writing with pen and paper???

Answer: It could, as a plan B. However, I'd suggest the old-school option of using pen and paper. There's something magical about it, and it makes you feel like the designer and architect of your life.

Question: What do you think is the biggest reason for scripting not working out for someone?

Answer: Scripting will not work if a person is using it out of desperation, like a quick fix or technique, without fully understanding the essential principles of making your mind work for you, choosing goals that excite you, staying motivated while enjoying the journey, and doing the inner work while re-designing your self-image.

Question: I'm a bit insecure about having a journal because I'm afraid someone from my family could casually find it and read it? I would feel so stupid! I know I could record my vision, but then once again, what if someone discovers it? They would think I'm going mad!

Answer: If you're into any kind of self-development, some people will indeed think you're going mad, haha. So, first of all, you need to ask yourself, what do you care about more? Your vision, success, and happiness? Or what will other people think of you? Now imagine, as you manifest your desires, your current negative voices that say, *"what will other people think of me"* might amplify accordingly. So, first things first, I would address the resistance and possible inner insecurities you are experiencing. The technique I would recommend you use is called the Emotional Freedom Technique (EFT). One of the best books I've read on this topic is called *The Tapping Solution* by Nick Ortner. I always recommend it to my readers because I know it can help them take care of their emotional wellbeing and eliminate resistance.

While I'm not an expert on EFT or a certified practitioner, I've been using it on myself successfully for over three years now and have experienced some tremendous shifts with it.

Hopefully, my answer will help you address what I believe might be the more profound issue preventing you from smooth manifestations.

To answer your question more practically, you could purchase a diary or journal with a lock; or save your journals in a locked safe. You have the right to protect your space!

Question: I found the perfect journal for my scripting journey, but it has some writing in it on the first page. Can I rip it out? Will it affect my manifestations?

Answer: You worry too much. If you feel good about the first page, keep it as it is. Maybe it was meant to be there as some kind of a lesson from the Universe. However, if it feels off, you can get rid of it. Honestly, I don't see any reason why it could affect your goals and manifestations in life.

Question: I know what to do. I know I logically understand how it all works. But I can't truly feel my vision. I'm very clear on my desires, I know what kind of career I want, and how big my new salary is. I know everything. But, I can't see my new self. I can't experience the feelings my new self would feel. So, I write and script, but I know I do it automatically, like a robot. I can still stick to it because I'm very disciplined, but I know it won't be effective because I can't seem to feel anything. Is there anything I can do to connect with my new self-image and experience all those unique feelings to manifest my desires faster?

Answer: Well done on successfully spotting what you might be doing wrong. You are an excellent LOA detective! And don't worry too much, because reconnecting with your feelings for manifestation purposes might take some time, especially if you are a very logical person (from the way you write, I would say you are, but you are also open to feelings and spirituality, which will really help you on your manifestation journey).

To help you, I recommend that you start using one of my favorite Law of Attraction Meditations from the next chapter.

Chapter 6

Powerful Law of Attraction Meditation to Connect with Your Higher Self

This meditation is designed to help you raise your vibration. So that you can align with the best version of yourself and mindfully attract your desires.

Sit down in a comfortable position. Take a few deep breaths.

Start off with a big, big smile. It's your time. Your time to shine. Your time to grow and expand.

So that you can manifest more of what you truly desire.

Inhale. Take a deep breath and imagine an ample white light. It's the light of all the possibilities. Allow it. Breathe it in, and feel it in all the cells of your body. It's the light from the Universe that can make all your wishes come true.

Now, peacefully allow yourself to exhale all your doubts and fears. Let go of all past judgments, blame, guilt, and self-criticism.

Carry on breathing deeply and slowly. But don't force it. You can choose to speed up or slow down. It's really up to you. Whatever feels right for you at this moment.

Breathe in the light and exhale the dark.

Remember that you are raising your vibration as you do this, therefore automatically attracting more highly vibrational experiences, people, and things into your life.

Now, take a moment to look back at your journey and be grateful for how far you have come. You've been learning. You've been growing. You've been expanding. Just give yourself a few moments to reflect on how much you have grown in the last year, two years, and five years.

Allow yourself to be grateful for all the challenges you overcame.

You've grown so much, and you are getting stronger and stronger with every second, minute, and hour.

Now you know what you desire. You know how to attract it. You are patient. You are enjoying the journey. And you choose to focus on positivity. Take a moment to feel thoroughly proud of yourself and how far you've come.

Now, you can allow yourself to look ahead. You are releasing all the doubts and negativity from the past. Remember to keep breathing in positive white light while breathing out what's no longer serving you on your journey.

Now, see the New You. The more empowered you. You from the future. How do you feel?

How do you speak and act?

Are you calmer and more at peace? Are you more confident and empowered?

Allow these positive feelings to light up in every cell of your body. How does it feel to be that future version of you already?

Be aware that to manifest faster, our focus should be on our personal and spiritual growth. We attract what we are.

You attract who you become. So, who are you?

Allow yourself to feel that person in every cell of your body. Be that person; right here and right now.

The next level version of you is now sitting right before you. You are smiling at one another. Your future is looking at you with so much love, compassion, and understanding. It wants to teach you and guide you.

What is the message Your Future You wants to tell you today?

Give your higher self a big, big hug and allow it to hug you back. You now merge and become one. You become your higher self. You are your higher self now.

Now, activate your new self and let go of whatever old identity no longer serves you.

Script to Manifest

Letting go is easy; simply say *goodbye* and release all negativity from the past.

Clench your fists tight and feel your fingers in your palms. This tension represents your old self, your old habits, actions, and beliefs. Old ways that were preventing you from shining your light. Your old mindsets and all the judgment, criticism, and fear.

Feel the effort that is required to hold you in that old place.

Now, unclench your fists. Feel the resistance and become aware of how easy it can be if you just let it go. Unclenching, relaxing, and living your life without tension, resistance, and old habits that no longer serve you feels so good.

Now, there is less effort and less tension, and your palms are open, so you are open to receiving more and more.

Open your fingers and allow every cell in your hands to start absorbing the new energy of abundance, love, and freedom. Feel that positive energy spread through your body.

Allow the energy to vibrate. Allow yourself to be empowered.

Wrap your arms around your shoulders and give yourself a hug. You are already ready to manifest your desires. You are already prepared to step into your dream life!

Give yourself a big hug.

Whisper: "*I am ready to receive*" to your heart.

Keep affirming: *"I am so proud of who I've become. I love the person I am now!"*

Take a deep inhale. Exhale and relax.

Also, remember you don't have to revert back to your old patterns. You have already merged with your new self. You are your unique self.

This is your real power. This is how amazing you are. Your higher self is right there with you. Your higher self is smiling at you now.

Whenever you feel worried or doubtful, visualize your higher self smiling at you and shining your light from within you.

Because it's you, it's who you indeed are!

Final words:

Keep practicing what you have learned, and keep sharing these concepts with others. Together we can change the world by collectively enhancing the vibration of the planet.

I genuinely hope that this book inspired you and gave you new tools to expand your consciousness and raise awareness.

You are limitless, you are powerful, and you are amazing!

I believe in you and wish you all the best on your journey!

Part 3 – Book 3

The LOVE of Attraction

Tested Secrets to Let Go of Fear-Based Mindsets, Activate LOA Faster, and Start Manifesting Your Desires!

By Elena G. Rivers

Copyright Elena G. Rivers © 2020

Why the LOVE of Attraction?

You can't fail with the power of love. Because love can create *only* good things in your life. So, if you're tired of negativity and feel ready to release what's no longer serving you so that you can start living your dream life, you've come to the right place.

You found this book for a reason! It doesn't matter if you've read any of my other books. It doesn't matter if you've studied or practiced LOA before. And it doesn't matter where you're from, how old you are and what you do for a living.

Anyone can unleash the power of love to release negative mindsets and energy patterns that block their positive manifestations.

This is why I'm writing this book! In the last few months, I've been getting signs from the Universe that made it clear I should write it. The signs would come consistently almost every day. Most readers who were reaching out to me seeking LOA guidance already knew a lot about it. They learned different manifestation methods and had some success with them. They even knew the Law of Attraction mistakes to avoid. Yet, for some reason, they still felt a little bit blocked. Judging from the way they wrote to me and asked questions, it became evident to me what the missing puzzle in their LOA practice was.

To take their manifestations to the next level, all they had to do was to embrace the power of love and authenticity. They had to use that power to get rid of all the negative mindsets and beliefs.

This book is short for a reason. It's not about how much time you spend reading (unless you really enjoy reading and it makes you feel good), but more about how you read and the time you take to apply what you've learned.

The introduction that follows will help you understand the fundamental pillars of this simple, love-based system. Then, we will jump into ten tested loved-based secrets to get you out of the negativity and into the spiral of positive manifestations.

The main thing I want you to understand is that *everything* you've been exposed to so far *is mostly fear-based*.

For example, what you hear on the news, advertising on social media, conversations you may have heard from other people. Most messages your mind receives are probably fear-based.

It's no wonder that our minds are so filled with fear. Even positive, spiritual people like us can still hold many fear-based mindsets.

And there is nothing wrong with realizing that. Conscious self-development is a journey that never ends. I release negativity almost every day!

If you've read any of my other books, you already know that I'm all for positivity. However, I'm not a big fan of fake positivity. I don't subscribe to burying your head in the sand, pretending all is good while actually feeling bad.

Genuine positivity and freedom emerge when we face our fear-based mindsets and energies while embracing a mindful state of awareness. Then, we can observe what's going on around us and mindfully choose a different, more aligned, and positive response. With a positive response from within, we change on a deeper level. Then, we have the power to influence our reality.

This is what this little book is designed to help you with. I highly recommend you get your notebook ready and do the exercises as you read. I also recommend you read this book several times. Every time you read the same book, the way you perceive it is different because every time you read it, your energy shifts.

So, without any further ado, let's do this!

As I already mentioned, we will start off with an introduction to understand how this love-based manifestation formula works.

Then, we will dive into ten powerful long-term manifestation secrets.

You can read this book in one sitting; it should take one or two hours max. Or, you can take your time and go through each secret every day. It's up to you!

I'm very excited for you and feel very privileged to be writing this book for you. My purpose in life is to help raise the vibration of the planet. I fulfill my mission mainly through writing, and I'm very grateful for curious, ambitious souls like you! Ambitious, spiritually curious people who are ready to take meaningful action, dive deeper, do the inner work, and become the change they want to see on this planet.

The Love of Attraction

"You must be the change you want to see in the world." – by Gandhi

"You can have everything in life you want if you will just help other people get what they want." – by Zig Ziglar

"People who have great lives think and talk about what they love more than what they don't love. And people who are struggling, think and talk about what they don't love more than what they do love." – by Rhonda Byrne

"Working on our own consciousness is the most important thing that we are doing at any moment, and being Love is the supreme creative act." – by Ram Dass

"The Law of Attraction or the Law of Love...they are one and the same." – by Charles Haanel

"If we look at the world with a love of life, the world will reveal its beauty to us." – by Daisaku Ikeda

The Love of Attraction

Why It's ALL About Mindfully Mastering the Basics

Do you know the secrets of the most successful football coaches? It's simple - they focus on the basic stuff before anything else. And even after getting into more advanced techniques, they always remind their students about the basics through consistent and mindful repetition.

They make sure their teams embrace the basics to such an extent that it becomes automatic to them.

For example, a football player can learn a myriad of new techniques to run faster and whatnot. However, if they can't even tie their shoes properly or have no clue how to prevent injury, they won't be successful.

Weird example, I know. But I see this all the time in LOA or self-help community. People are looking for some magic pill or for something new.

The truth is that it's not about how much we know. Yes, knowledge is power. I don't discredit the desire for more knowledge. But, what's even more power is your expertise in action. You want your ability to turn into your inner wisdom. So that all your efforts, thoughts, and feelings are aligned with what you desire.

To get to that level, it's all about mindful repetition of what you already know. Even when it feels a bit boring.

And trust me, I learned this the hard way!

It's up to you to make it exciting by using your imagination. Why am I telling you this?

Well, have you considered grounding yourself before diving into this material? Do you ever ground yourself? And do you ground yourself every day?

If you don't because you've never heard of it, and you don't know how, well, you will start in just a minute. But, if you already know what grounding is, but you don't do it, use it as a signal from the Universe to ground yourself more often. Don't be one of those negative, sarcastic "LOA-ers" who just complain about everything they read with: "Oh, nothing new here."

I used to be one of those sarcastic "I already know it all" individuals too. I struggled with weight loss for years, and I just kept reading more fad diet books. I would criticize all of them. *Nothing new here!* It was only when someone called me bitter and fat that I actually decided to do something about my weight.

Instead of looking for a new diet plan or a magic pill, I focused on the basics. I stopped eating fast food and drinking soda. I quit sugar and began walking every day. That little lifestyle change alone helped me lose weight! A simple, common-sense diet and moderate exercise.

Now, I'm very grateful for my weight loss struggle because it taught me how to be a better person and release sarcasm. Now, I really appreciate anyone who puts themselves out there with any material designed to help people with something.

Even if I'm already familiar with their information, or it's not really for me, I still appreciate their efforts. Why? Because now, I operate from a place of love, not fear, criticism, and jealousy. And so, even if I'm to give someone honest feedback that I believe can help them improve, I do it kindly and with respect.

We're not necessarily looking for the new. Instead, we're unleashing something that deep inside we know is good for us. We make a mindful decision to do what we already know, again and again, to use it as a personal transformation tool.

This is why I politely ask you to please ground yourself first to get the most out of this book.

(And everything you read or do, really.)

The Love of Attraction

One of my best friends is a professional saleswoman who did very well in her career. She grounds herself before most of her sales calls. Her energy is better because of her simple grounding rituals, and she gets much better results with her work.

I ground myself before all my writing sessions, and now I never experience the so-called *writer's block*. When you ground yourself, are calm, and operate from a place of love and authenticity, there is no such thing as *a block*.

Doing your work feels right and natural—no reason to block anything.

OK, so let's ground! I'm here right now grounding myself with you!

The Love of Attraction

Grounding Exercise
(Just Do It and Please Don't Complain You Already Know This!)

Take off your shoes. Relax Your Body.

Close your eyes.

Start breathing consciously.

Breathe in for 3-5 seconds, hold your breath for 3-5 seconds, and then breathe out for 3-5 seconds.

Repeat several times until you start feeling relaxed.

Keep breathing consciously at whatever pace is convenient for you.

Now, get in a flow state by imagining light from the sky, beautiful, warm yellow light, enter your body through your head. You can feel the light warming your head and moving down and down, illuminating all your body.

Now, the light reaches your feet, going deeper and deeper. Visualize the light diving deep into the earth and becoming a grounding root.

Finish off your grounding process by saying thank you, thank you, thank you.

This short exercise shouldn't take more than five minutes. I highly recommend you do it whenever you need to enter a peaceful state of mind or raise your awareness and learn new things better and faster.

I want you to remember that this yellow light is always there for you. Whenever you need to wash off any negative feelings or experiences; whenever you need to make a decision or do something important but feel unfocused - get back to doing this exercise.

Love is the creative force of everything in the Universe.

And it's the only force that can permanently take you from fear, negativity, and darkness to manifesting your dream life, almost on autopilot. It's not even about how many manifestation methods you know or do. It's about who you are and who you become. Your energy and vibration are everything. When you turn to love and embody love, you will automatically manifest everything that you love.

Before I discovered the Love of Attraction, my life was a mess. Yes, I kept manifesting, but only negative things. I manifested a very abusive relationship. I lacked the courage to leave because I felt scared of being alone and feared that nobody would want me because I was too old.

I manifested a job and then my own business that most people would envy. Unfortunately, it wasn't aligned with my passions and strengths and would always burn me out.

Even with a good salary, I always lacked money. I felt scared because some unexpected expenses would always manifest, and I couldn't get out of debt.

I couldn't experience vibrant health either. Even though I tried to stay healthy, my stressful life eventually led me to resort to alcohol, fast food, tobacco, and other substances to numb myself. I couldn't stick to any self-care plan. And as you already know, I struggled with weight loss. It felt like all the old energies and emotions I couldn't release kept accumulating as excess weight.

It wasn't until I decided to dive deep to examine the root cause of all my problems that a sad but very liberating realization came:

Elena, you're living your life and making all decisions from a place of fear, not a place of love. You're in the mindset and energy of escaping from what you don't want. You keep focusing on the negative. Therefore, you negatively activate the

The Love of Attraction

Law of Attraction. Focus on love. Make decisions from a place of love and love yourself to start attracting people and circumstances that love you.

Then, I took meaningful action and decided to work on myself using love-based concepts of the Law of Attraction, which I now call the LOVE of Attraction.

Just a few months after my decision, I transformed every area of my life. I was no longer in an abusive relationship; I found my way out and was happily single.

At that time, I wanted to focus on healing myself and doing the inner work before repeating my old patterns of "trying to find someone to not feel alone." So, being single is what I wanted back then. And eventually, I did manifest my soul mate and moved to a beautiful island in the Atlantic.

I found the courage to finally be myself and follow my passion with love and confidence. My new energy opened several new professional gates for me, such as manifesting an unexpected deal with an audiobook company. Now, I love the work I'm doing, and even though I work hard, I no longer feel burned out. It all feels very aligned, and I'm honored to be fulfilling my life mission and purpose every day.

My health improved because I embraced the power of love and self-care. Instead of taking misaligned actions from the fear of getting overweight or sick, I took action from a place of love for healthy living. It felt natural to me to eat a whole-food diet and highly vibrational foods. That gave me more energy and conviction to carry on.

And, most importantly, I began attracting super high vibe people into my life. This is what I call *true abundance-* when all areas of your life are aligned and complement one another.

After all, would you like to manifest vast amounts of money but end up sick, unhappy, or unfulfilled? Of course not. You want abundance in all areas of your life.

So, take a few minutes now to reflect. You, too, can design your ideal life from a place of love, not fear. Yes, there's always one area of life that might need more attention.

But, staying in balance is essential. You want to create abundance! Not only in terms of dollars made. Your emotional bank account balance also matters.

Design a vision for your dream life now and create a short mission statement (one to three sentences) for each area of your life:

My health

Example:
-*I choose to eat healthy foods that give me unstoppable energy and vibrant health.*

-*I love foods that nourish my body.*

-*I'm blessed to indulge in long baths and beautiful walks in nature.*

My Passion/ Purpose / Fulfillment

Example:

-*I feel so grateful I found my calling in life.*

-*I'm even more grateful I can do my passion for a living.*

-*My purpose sets my soul on fire!*

My relationships

Example:

-I get amazingly well with my family, friends, and the man/woman of my dreams.

-We're all happy people; we love and support each other.

-I attract high vibe people into my life.

Money/finance

Example:

-I'm open to receiving.

-I mindfully create new opportunities and new sources of income.

-Money is energy, and I'm energy; therefore, I attract money into my life.

Spirituality

Example:

-I experience unforgettable spiritual moments in my life.

- I feel loved and cared for by the Universe/God/ Higher Power.

That was the first step. Get back to it to remind yourself what's yet to come and how amazing your life can get.

Everything happens for a reason, and there are no coincidences. We attracted each other. After experiencing my own personal transformation, I made it my mission to help others do the same. Our planet needs more love and more loved-based people. And so, my intention is to awaken those who are still in a fear-based mindset so that they can awaken to the creative power of love.

But you must be open to receiving help. You see, so many people I know asked me for help because they saw my transformation. But when I explained what I did, they began saying:

Oh, you just got lucky.

Or:

It's because you were in the right place at the right time.

Or:

It's because you were born rich.

Which is not true. My transformation did not happen by accident. And I wasn't born into a wealthy or influential family either.

What happened is that I took concrete steps to change my actions, feelings, responses, and thoughts. As a curious mind, I reverse-engineered what worked and created my own Love of Attraction formula.

Those who asked me for help and were open to receiving support didn't discredit my transformation as some coincidence. Instead, they happily followed the exact same process, in their own way. As a result, they, too, could transform all areas of their lives.

Take a look at your dream life vision you've designed in the previous exercise. Ask yourself, do you really desire to attract all that? Would you be open to making your vision a reality or get closer to your goals in the next few months?

If the answer is yes, keep reading and applying. This guide is not designed for passive reading, and I can't help those who are skeptical and aren't willing to follow the steps I outlined.

The Love of Attraction

I still remember how embarrassing it felt...it was my birthday. I invited some friends over. I went to the store to buy some food and drinks for my party, and my credit card got declined. I had to leave with nothing. I can still remember how embarrassing it felt! All those people at the supermarket were staring at me.

Then, I discovered I didn't even have enough gas to drive back home. I had to ask friends for help. I felt ashamed to share my situation with my family or partner. All I could attract was debt. And it was back then when I hit my rock bottom that I just knew I had to change myself and my energy.

LOA and manifestation saved me. To be more precise, the Love of Attraction saved me.

Everything has its vibrational energy. This page has a vibration, and so does your hand. Your thoughts and emotions are energy, and they also stimulate the release of neurohormones, which send signals to your brain.

The grey matter, the part of the brain that controls your emotions, impulses, and thoughts, is something we can influence, using the positive power of love.

We can control our emotional responses to external stimuli and events. In other words-we can send positive, loved-based frequencies towards our desires so that we don't get pushed off course with misaligned frequencies.

For example, if someone is rude to you, what is your response? Are you angry the entire day? Or do you allow yourself a few minutes to process that negativity and then consciously take meaningful action to get back to a positive vibration? Do you deviate your energy just because something didn't go well? Or do you decide to move on because you know that even if things don't go as planned, the Universe knows what's right for your long-term wellbeing?

When you decide to focus on conscious decisions, you become a conscious person. As a conscious person, you create conscious life. You design your life just like you already did!

It's all about understanding and then removing old programs and blueprints that might be leading you to negative manifestations. Awareness is so important.

There are seven crucial pillars in this process. We will have a look at each of them so that you understand how it works. Then, we will be diving into ten Love of Attraction secrets. But before we do, it's so important you understand the framework! Mindset is everything!

Pillar #1 Your Authentic Alignment

Understand that if you choose so, everything happens for you, not to you. Sometimes things don't go our way because there's something better waiting for us. The Universe knows what's good for us.

Sometimes it just wants to test us or send us challenging circumstances for us to transform. For example, I'm grateful for all the hardship I'd experienced. I see it as a blessing because this is how I hit rock bottom and decided to transform. Many people experience something very similar.

Ask yourself, how do you react when things don't go your way? For example, you wanted to manifest a new job or promotion but didn't get it. You can choose to feel scared or pessimistic: *why me? Why can others do it and I can't? What's wrong with me?*

Or, you can choose to affirm to the Universe: *Thank you for testing me, I'm still here, and I know I'm on the right path. Thank you for the reminder!*

Pillar #2 Your Desire Must be Authentic and So Must Be Your Energy

Very often, we set goals that aren't even ours but come from other people. In other words, we want to manifest and achieve to make other people happy or to show off. I've been there so many times, and for so long, I had no idea I was blocking my own happiness.

The honest truth is that with no authenticity, there is no alignment. And with no alignment, we can't manifest positive outcomes. No matter how hard we try.

Whatever it is that you set to manifest, it must be your goal. Suppose you want something simply because everyone else has it, and you don't want to be left behind. In that case, you are following trends, not your true authentic desires. Keep asking your higher self: *is this what I truly want? Will it make me happy?*

Pillar #3 Process Negative Energy Fast

What do you do when you encounter a negative block, person, or situation? For example, someone said something rude to you. How much time do you need to let go? Five seconds, five hours, five days, fifty years?

The sooner you let go, the better. Understand that rude people harm themselves, not you.

You can choose to stay out of their negative vibration.

Also, by doing the inner work described in this guide, you will be raising your vibration, attracting more positive people, and automatically moving away from fear.

The art of letting go is so crucial. Whenever I experience something negative, I allow myself some time to process and release it.

With practice and firm intention, it becomes automatic. The more you hold onto negative things that someone did to you, the more you harm yourself. You keep replaying the negative loop and experiencing the same negative vibration over and over again.

The Love of Attraction

And when it comes to rude people and their negativity, well, it's theirs. Choose to hold your space. Visualize yourself having a nice shower in a waterfall. Keep breathing and affirming: *I fly so high that I can only see positivity.*

Pillar #4 Love vs. Fear-Based Mindset

Jessica desires to manifest a beach house because she loves the vibe of the ocean. She loves the seagulls and surfing. She feels free, waking up near the ocean. So, she manifests from a place of love. For her, manifesting a beach house fully aligns with who she is.

However, Mary wants to manifest a beach house because one of her siblings lives in one. Her parents keep praising her sibling and their successful professional career and how they could afford such a place. Mary doesn't feel appreciated by her parents. So, she thinks that by manifesting a beach house, she too will get attention and appreciation. She imagines how it would feel to invite some of her friends to her new home and how they would envy her such a success. Maybe she could even get a bigger house than her sibling.

Needless to say, Jessica manifests from a loved-based mindset and Mary from a fear-based mindset. Which manifestation do you think will have a happy ending? By a happy ending, I refer to a lifetime of joy, fulfillment, and abundance.

I used to be so similar to Mary! I was in constant fear and wanted to prove to others that I was worthy, smart, and significant. Yet, I couldn't believe it myself. I wasn't myself. My goals weren't mine.

So, ask yourself, do you want to manifest from a place of love or fear? Misaligned mindsets come from anxiety and other people's opinions. Don't allow them into your space.

Don't hold onto the stuck energy of trying to please other people and manifest to show off. Stuck energy leads to bad circumstances. Don't manifest from fear; fear isn't yours. Be aware that fear-based goals may hide in superficial prestige, appreciation, and desperate attempts to make other people like you.

When you think about what you desire to manifest, you should feel light, not heavy. Too much heavy energy indicates that what you wish to manifest is not truly yours, or you're not ready for it yet. For the time being, you should prepare yourself by doing something else.

Your emotions hold super strong frequency. They eventually manifest into a physical reality by going from fluid to dense. Suppose you focus on positive emotions and use all their power. In that case, you will automatically manifest more positive things into your life.

The Love of Attraction

Unfortunately, most people use this formula but with negative emotions and get stuck in a never-ending negative loop.

Pillar #5 Know Your Authentic Frequency

Some people don't study LOA and manifestation, yet they always manifest incredible things. Why is that?

Well, some people have this natural, positive energy, and they've been filled with it for a long time. They just align, take action, and get what they desire. And, most importantly, they are authentic, and they know what they want. They don't confuse the Universe.

In contrast, some people, such as my old self, have no idea about their authentic desires and try to manifest to please other people. Or they desire things because it's a trend and everyone is doing this or having that.

Be that simple, authentic, and aligned person. It's a choice. Less is more. You can start manifesting one desire at a time if you fully embrace the energy of positive emotion and authentic love.

Be true to yourself and always speak your truth from a place of kindness, consideration, and respect for others whose truth might be different. It's not that we all have to believe in the same things. It's all about allowing yourself and others to live in peace.

Pillar #6 Release Wanting and Doubting

If you struggle with manifesting, chances are your energy is split in two or more directions.

For example, maybe you desire to manifest your own brand. You want to be a revolutionary coach, have an online presence, and attract amazing clients.

A business mentor advises you to start a YouTube channel to share your truth, provide value, and attract those who seek guidance. Or perhaps you're advised to start running Facebook ads.

Yet, you're scared…what if your friends and family see your videos or advertisements and they don't like them? And so, your energy is split.

We often split our energy subconsciously, we want something consciously, but deep inside, we fear it. For example, you may think you want money (deliberately). Still, your subconscious mind rebels thinking it's evil, and you might lose your friends. And so, since all your actions are led by your subconscious, you start sabotaging yourself.

No judgment here; negative results are just feedback. They are not even that negative if we use them correctly- as a motivation to shed light on the darkness while releasing old beliefs that no longer serve us. You don't fail, you succeed, or you learn. Treat unfavorable circumstances as data. Imagine you're a mad LOA detective or scientist; well, now you know what not to do!

Pillar #7 When Focusing on "Why Not's" Can Be Good for You

Go back to your dream life exercise. If you're not living it right now, ask yourself, why can't you have it? Did someone say something in the past, making you feel unworthy?

For example, for years, I struggled in business because my ex-partner once told me:

So, you want to start your own business? You're a cute wannabie. Yeah, right, like one of those femalepreneur lady bosses posing on social media. I saw one offering a webinar today. Laughable! They know nothing about business, and you know even less than they do. You're so cute talking about it, but you're not cut out for business. Business is men's stuff. And what when we settle down and have kids? You're not gonna have time for your business anyway".

And for years, it was my story, a man told me this, and I chose to believe it. I didn't even consciously remember I made it my belief.
So, if something similar happened to you, release it now! Everything is possible with the love of attraction because love is the highest power that can arrange everything for your highest good, happiness, and abundance!

Use the following questions:
-*what do you want?*
-*why do you think you can't have it now?*
-*is it your belief or rule or someone else's*
-*where did you get those rules?*
-*does this old baggage empower you in any way?*

Misaligned energy is used to protect your old ways that perhaps were helpful in the past. But now, unfortunately, they close new channels of abundance and happiness for you.

Keep affirming to the Universe that you're ready for and open to new possibilities and new avenues of receiving for the highest good of all.

Now that you understand the foundation of love versus fear-based mindsets and how to use their power to activate LOA while releasing negativity, let's jump into our love-based secrets. Each secret focuses on a specific technique, question, or exploration to turn your life into a never-ending flow of love and abundance in all areas of your life.

Secret #1 Realize When Your Subconscious Mind Goes Against You and Change the Disk

Kate is a gorgeous woman. Yet, she always struggled with her self-image. She was obsessed with her looks, always looking for ways to "improve" and look better.

Yet, whenever someone complimented her, she didn't take it seriously; she thought they were ironic or trying to get to her.

She struggled with relationships too. For some reason, the men she liked would always choose other women (who, for some reason, weren't that astonishingly beautiful). Everyone would say that poor Kate simply "didn't have luck" in love. And that all those men were stupid for not wanting to be with her.

The negative pattern would continue. Kate tried to look more beautiful (even though she was already beautiful). But, for some reason, she kept repelling all the men she liked. She was living a life of loneliness and not feeling good enough.

Eventually, she embarked on a self-development journey and learned how to dive deep. She wanted to find the root cause of all her issues.

The Love of Attraction

It turned out that when she was a little girl, a family member called her ugly.

And that event stayed in her subconscious mind for years. At first, it was there, like a dormant volcano. But, when Kate was a teenager, she began obsessing with her looks, realizing that she needed compliments from other people to feel worthy.

The negative pattern got re-activated and haunted her for years. Only when she understood the fear-based mechanism that was driving her for so many years could she do something about it.

She could finally, as I like to put it, change the disk.

Or, in other words, she could change her behavior. She could accept the fact she didn't need to prove anything to anyone. She was already naturally beautiful and could own her beauty. She no longer had to resort to plastic surgeries and enhancements to "keep improving." She could be herself. As such, she attracted an amazing man into her life.

What about you and your old disk? What negative patterns do you hold about your:

-looks
-qualifications
-finances

-relationships

What is the fear-based program that's controlling your life and your behaviors?

Are you ready to let it go for good? There's time to hold on, and there's time to let go. When letting go of any negative pattern or fear-based belief, embrace self-love as much as you can.

It's common for many people (and I've been there myself too) to feel angry, guilty, or even stupid when thinking about their old behaviors.

Embrace the power of mindfulness and the present moment. Take a few deep breaths. At this moment, you are safe and empowered. You write your own story. You design your life.

Keep affirming:

I'm now safe.

There's time to hold on, and there's time to let go.

Hey, my subconscious mind, I want to thank you for holding on to this belief (that I wasn't good enough, was fat, wasn't beautiful enough).

The Love of Attraction

I know you were trying to protect me.

But now, it's time for me to let go. From now on, I choose to believe that I'm good enough, I'm worthy of love, abundance, and financial freedom.

For many people, this is the missing link to the Law of Attraction. Creating your own affirmations that make friends with your subconscious mind.

Thank your subconscious mind for trying to protect you for so many years. Kindly let it know that now times have changed - you're safe, and you can now choose a different set of beliefs, therefore acting differently.

At the same time, many people choose positive thinking, which is excellent. However, they are still driven by their old behaviors because they haven't made friends with their subconscious mind. They haven't changed the disk, or in other words, they haven't changed their actions and how they react to different situations.

This was my story, too, for so many years. Yes, I felt a bit better because of "trying to stay positive." But I was still the old me, trying to prove myself to others all the time because I didn't feel worthy. Like I mentioned previously, an ex-partner of mine ridiculed my ideas of having my own business. And so, later, all my actions were driven by the fact that I wanted to show him and others that I could succeed in business (even if the price was to go against my own happiness).

Fear-based motivations are very short-sighted. Yes, they can help us get started on a new path. But they will not allow us to keep going while living happy, balanced, and abundant lives.

Ask yourself if you're ready to change your behavior and how you react to different situations. The Love of Attraction is not only about how you think but also about how you act. Suppose you really change the way you think. In that case, it means you automatically become a different person and change the way you act, therefore creating a new reality.

Secret #2 Do You Choose to Feel Light or Heavy?

You have your internal compass, your intuition. You are the only one who can make accurate decisions in alignment with who you are.

Before we dive deeper, please note, the purpose of this section is not to make you feel bad. I don't want you to go on any guilt trips such as: "Oh no, all the decisions or most of the decisions I made in my life were made out of fear."

Here's the truth: we all made most of our life decisions based on fear because this is how we were programmed. There's no point in feeling bad. If anything, you can choose to feel liberated because now you can stick to love-based mindsets and change your life.

An authentic decision is when you feel light. You know you are choosing something in alignment with your true desires. For example, you decide to follow your passion and sign up for a certified program to become a life coach. You follow your intuition. You just know you're doing the right thing.

At the same time, if you decide to make other people happy (even though you feel totally out of alignment), you might experience heaviness.

Heaviness is caused by fear-based mindsets. Perhaps you make a decision totally against yourself because you were told that things "have always been done in a certain way." Or maybe your decision is automatic; you don't even give it much thought because you have no idea what's driving you.

If you want to live a happy life, most of your decisions need to be made out of love and in alignment with your authentic goals and aspirations.

I use the word "most" because I'm a realist. And I know that not everything is black or white. For example, in some cases, we need a little bit of fear-based motivation to get started on taking action or to realize we need to change. There's nothing wrong with short-term fear-based measures if they are meant to lead us to our light. Everyone is on a different journey. Simultaneously, to get into alignment and follow our inner light, sometimes we need to face our demons and fear-based mindsets, which can feel a bit heavy.

But, once again, that initial heaviness and fear-based feelings eventually dissolve into love and light.

The Love of Attraction

Set the intention to simply become aware of when you feel light and when you feel heavy.

Whenever you feel heavy, ask yourself *why*? Is it because you take fear-based actions that are out of alignment with who you are? Or is it because you take action to make others happy?

Or perhaps you experience that initial feeling of heaviness only because you're facing your inner demons? And learning the truth about the love and fear-based mindsets result in overwhelm?

Remember that, whatever happened, happened. You were a different person back then. But now, you can choose to make decisions out of love and design your life out of love!

Secret #3 Choosing Your Vibration

Most people choose to live in the past, and they allow harmful programs to control their lives. But now, you know you can choose to live with love.

From now on, choose to perceive your reality differently. Instead of thinking of the world as some random and cruel place that is against you and sends you unfavorable circumstances all the time ("Oh no, something is wrong with me, why do I always attract the negative!"), you can perceive whatever happens around you as feedback.

Many readers ask me: *OK, so, I've been living consciously, thinking, and acting positively. I'm aware of the negative patterns that used to hold me back, and I keep releasing them. I know I'm acting differently. Yet, quite often, I still experience the old situations and circumstances in my life. Why is that?*

First of all, there is always a delay from the Universe. Which explains why so many people give up on the Law of Attraction. They run out of patience to carry on changing their thoughts, feelings, and actions.

Let's say a person was in a negative, fear-based mindset all their life. Now, at forty-something years old, they are eager to change. And they do change. It's January the 1st, and as a part of their New Year's resolutions, they consciously apply love, light, and LOA.

Yet, a few months pass, it's now April, and even though a person feels better and more positive, their reality still hasn't changed that much.

Or perhaps it did shift, but not as much as they expected it to. And once again, everything is a choice. A person can choose to think that LOA doesn't work, and it wasn't worth it. All that time they put into reading and changing themselves, they could have just hung out at the bar and keep complaining about their life.

But at the same time, a person can choose to accept that whatever happens inside and around them is just feedback from the Universe! Negative emotions can be feedback. And unfavorable circumstances can also be feedback.

If you genuinely embrace LOA and a love-based mindset, you know and understand that real transformation takes time; you need patience.

At the same time, you need to consciously focus on the fact that you are continually getting signals from the Universe.

For example, you asked for money and abundance. You were excited to set up a new business; it all started so well. But then, a few months pass. You had a bad month, and your revenue went down.

You can choose to feel negative.

You can also use it as feedback from the Universe, such as: *perhaps I could create another stream of revenue for my business? Maybe there's another way I could use to attract clients? Could I use this situation as a motivation to improve my marketing?*

The light is always there if you're willing to look for it!

Let me share another example from my own life…

At the beginning of this year, I asked the Universe for energy and vibrant health because I wanted the strength and stamina to write several new books. Yet, a couple of months after I'd formulated my wish, I got very sick.

And yes, it's our human nature to automatically choose fear and complaining. For a few days, I began doubting myself, LOA, and my own teachings.

How can this be? I had a vision; I did everything that LOA tells us to do, and instead of vibrant health, I got the opposite?

But then, I decided to use my circumstances as feedback from the Universe. I understood that the Universe wanted me to slow down. I really had to take my health seriously.

I had to take a few months off, which seemed scary at first (after all, I wanted to manifest more money and abundance, which is why I asked for energy and health!). But eventually, I understood that it all happened for me, not to me. And now, a year after my initial request, I finally have the energy and vibrant health I wanted. I really had to learn to slow down.

I had to get sick first to get serious about my health and go on a holistic self-care journey. Now, I'm a different person. My health habits changed, my diet changed. In other words: my initial unfavorable circumstances lovingly forced me to take better care of myself.

The Love of Attraction

I've seen similar patterns all over again, in different people who asked for love, abundance, health, or money and were given some kind of a test from the Universe.

Remember, whatever happens inside and around you, it's just feedback. And you can always consciously choose to raise your vibration by understanding that everything happens for you.

Rude boss? Well, you can now have more motivation to be a kind person and treat others with love.

Did you get sick? Well, your body is sending you an important message. It really needs some rest.

The relationship you're in is not what you hoped it would be. Well, perhaps now you genuinely understand the qualities of your dream partner?

Make it your daily mantra: *It all happens for me. Everything is unfolding just like it should.*

Some negative situations may sometimes manifest because of old, fear-based mindsets you held onto for so many years. It's OK, no judgment. It's just a reminder of how far you've come. Stick to love and light. All you have is the present moment. It's the present moment that creates a new, better future for you and your loved ones!

The Love of Attraction

Secret #4 The Power of the Why Behind the Why

By embracing a love-based mindset, you become a conscious detective of your life. You always strive to find the root cause of any negativity or negative feeling in your life.

For example, you get late to work, because there was traffic. Most people would just say: *Oh, I'm having a bad day, and I guess my whole week will be like that.*

However, you can ask yourself: *why do I think I'm having a bad day? What happened?*

And you may start to uncover some answers such as:

I found the traffic very annoying because most people seemed so rude and uncaring. I felt like the whole world was against me, trying to make me late for work.

OK, so how exactly did I feel?

Well, I felt very powerless. No matter what I do, I can't get to work on time, and I feel stupid. Then, I'm late, and my boss and colleagues think I'm not serious. What if they laugh at me or tell me to leave?

Why would they ask me to leave if I'm never late to work, I'm good at what I do, there was an accident on the road, and for the first time in many years, I was fifteen minutes late?

Oh...because once as a teen, I missed the school bus and arrived late, and the teacher asked me to leave.

And from then on, he would never take me seriously...No matter how hard I studied.

BOOM! Now you can take a few deep breaths and allow yourself to be *authentically you* again. You are safe now. What happened, happened. Focus on the present moment. Nobody wants to put you down or make you leave. Instead, you were presented with a situation that helped you unpeel some negative emotions from the past and release old feelings of guilt.

Whenever you feel bad, use it as an opportunity to learn more about yourself and what triggers you. Play your own LOA detective! You're always learning more about yourself and the world around you!

Secret #5 Releasing Low Vibrations and Using Certainty for Your Highest Good

This little secret consists of two parts. The first one is based on understanding your emotional state and needs.

Your life is all about your emotional frequency. When you intend to create something in your life, you're going after a specific emotional state in reality.

If you manifest from an authentic state, you should access pure and honest vibrational energy.

For example, let's say you desire to manifest a new job and feel very passionate about it. You've researched the company you want to work for. You really love what they're doing and want to be a part of their team. Your energy is authentic. You feel good even before manifesting your desire. You feel excited, just thinking about it. At the same time, you already feel whole and complete. You're grateful for the work you're doing now and simply choose to upgrade your professional life from a place of love and excitement.

And with authentic energy, you manifest not only faster but also with joy and ease. What you manifest really makes you happy and transforms your life.

But, if your intentional energy is rooted in lack, you want to manifest to then feel whole and complete. It's a fear-based mindset because you assume that unless you don't manifest what you want, you can't feel happy. And so, you keep manifesting negative patterns of waiting and hoping for something to happen to then make you feel good and worthy.

Remove attachment by creating the feeling first. What emotional states are you trying to get through your manifestations? Can you feel them now?

When you think about your goal, what negative thoughts and voices come to your mind?

Create a pure connection by embracing all the positive and loved-based mindsets associated with your manifestation.

Let's say you want a beautiful house. At the same time, you want real, love-based friends who appreciate who you are. You also want financial security so that you don't need to worry about paying for the house.

The Love of Attraction

Well, to create a union of good feelings and a clear signal for the Universe, you can visualize yourself in your dream house, with your dream friends, having a good time. You can then visualize yourself at your friends' houses. You all have lovely homes, it's normal for you. Nobody is jealous. All your friends are happy and abundant.

At the same time, if you try to manifest a new house, because right now you don't like your current one, or feel ashamed to invite your friends over...well... you're trying to manifest from a place of fear.

Or perhaps you want to manifest a beautiful house to feel significant? Well, why do you want to feel significant? Do you want to manifest from a place of love for a new home? Or do you fear that other people might think you're not good or successful enough unless you manifest something that impresses them?

Before intending to manifest anything, the bottom line is: you need to get rid of negative vibrations.
Negative vibrations come from fear. And to manifest our deepest desires, we need to step into unlimited love for ourselves, those around us, and our manifestations.

The second part of this secret is understanding your need for certainty while using it for your good, from a place of love.

The Love of Attraction

Humans always want to feel safe to have something to count on. Our brain is always looking for ways to survive, not necessarily thrive or have an extraordinary life.

When you wake up and decide to live in expansion, you need to release the need for certainty if it comes from low vibrations and fear.

For example, people who get stuck in abusive relationships or jobs they hate often choose to stay where they are because it fulfills their need for certainty.

People who choose to eat fast food also do so because of certainty. There's a certainty of some flavors, maybe the need for sugar rush.

Now, there is nothing wrong with craving certainty.
Unless you choose a life of constant travel and adventure, you probably require certainty too. You want to make a certain amount of money a month. You want to know your work schedule. You want to be in a steady and loving relationship.

All you need to do is upgrade your needs; you can meet a need for certainty differently. You can find a new job that you love, and that also gives you confidence. You can have a loving partner that also fulfills your needs for certainty.

The Love of Attraction

Your need for love and financial stability can be satisfied in a healthy, love-based way.

Revise your need for certainty. What's your next step? Is there a better, healthier way? There's always an answer.

Secret #6 Not All Negative Programming Is Really Negative

There's always good in bad. Most self-help and LOA literature talks about "programming" as something terrible, something we need to release at all costs. And yes, in most cases, it makes sense.

But we need to remember that there's negative programming as well as positive programming. Also, you may be running a good program for you and your current situation right now. However, it may turn out not to be longer beneficial for your new goals or levels of awareness in the future.

This is important to understand to save you negative feelings of shame and guilt!

There's a pattern amongst people who decide to do some inner work. They uncover negative patterns and programs that used to control their past behavior, and now they feel bad about themselves or start resenting other people.

Once again, remember, there's time to hold on, and there's time to let go. Perhaps you wanted to become an artist, and you realized that what was holding you back was a harmful program from the past. A relative told you that your work wasn't good enough. Now, you keep running that memory in your mind, feeling resentment toward that person and feeling guilty you took their words seriously.

Once again, don't torture yourself. There's no need to run the same situation in your mind over and over again. Maybe the family member had good intentions; they honestly said they thought that you weren't ready. They didn't say you weren't good enough but that your work back then wasn't good enough.

In other words, they had good intentions.

Now, it's up to you. You can turn that negative program into something positive; for example, *a family member tried to protect me from disappointment. They wanted me to practice more. They didn't want me to hear too many negative remarks from art critics.*

When you choose to transform negative into positive, your whole vibration changes. Now, you're genuinely empowered and can follow your path.

Or perhaps, you're running a program that you think is positive, but it turns out to be a bit misleading. You think you are already good enough to quit your job and become self-employed. When you were a kid, everyone always praised you for everything and was very supportive.

So, you keep running this program and quit your job, cold turkey. You feel confident you'll be able to make a good living as self-employed.

But it soon turns out that you can't find enough clients and aren't genuinely ready yet to be a full-time entrepreneur.

What you thought was a positive program turns out to be a bit negative because it doesn't get you closer to your goals. You realize you still don't have enough skills to make a living as a self-employed person.

And once again, you can resent your family because of the old programs they gave you ("you're the best," "you can do everything you want"). You can choose to feel like you've made a fool out of yourself.

Or you can mindfully decide to choose a new program. The old program you got from your family was useful for you when you were a kid. Your family had good intentions. They wanted you to feel confident enough to see what you were capable of.

Now, you can choose to feel thankful. At least you tested what it would feel like to be self-employed. Thanks to that, you now know what you need to focus on to succeed when you're ready to become a full-time entrepreneur.

The Love of Attraction

The Universe gives you whatever vibration you're sending out. So, suppose you resent yourself and others because of some old program that turned out to be negative. In that case, the Universe will keep sending you more people, memories, and circumstances you can resent.

Release shame and guilt. Embrace the power of understanding. Stop criticizing yourself and others. Nobody is perfect. Yes, maybe your grandma gave you a negative belief about money, love, or something else. But, most likely, she had good intentions and wanted to protect you.

Explore your beliefs about money, love, career, friendships. Write down all the old, harmful programs, and simply set the intention to release them.

I also recommend you start practicing cord-cutting. You can cut cords with a person, feeling, old belief, and old energies that hold you back from living your full potential.

Even if you don't know the *what*, *who*, and *when*, you just feel like some negative energy is blocking you, but you don't know why, cord-cutting can also help you.

So, here's how you can cut cords with people, events, old timelines, feelings, objects, negative energies...whatever keeps you away from your vision!

Start by visualizing the individual, place, event, or feeling you wish to cut a cord with. Then, imagine scissors so that you can cut the cord.

(For example, if you continuously feel a negative feeling, and it keeps coming up in your visualizations, but you don't know whether it was a person who caused it, or perhaps an event, you can visualize the feeling, give it a color, shape or form and then cut cords with it).

Begin by connecting to the energy of the Divine — or the source.

Visualize the energetic cord that connects you with the low vibration entity you want to let go of.

Feel the energy that this entity is taking from you.

Now, set the intention to let go and visualize yourself cutting the cord between you and the negative entity using imaginary scissors.

Visualize the energetic cords recoil back.

Now, feel the recovery of energy and thank the other entity for their role in your life. Anchor that feeling of freedom and energy by pressing your thumb and index finger together.

The Love of Attraction

To amplify this experience, you may choose to say (or think) the following words:

I now finally release all energetic cords because they no longer serve me.

I release you, and I remove me from these binds.

All cords are destroyed, across all dimensions, times, and planes, never to return.

I now banish these energetic cords and recover now all energy that was once lost.

My energy flows back to me, filling me once again with vitality and creating now a peaceful, energetic boundary of love and light.

Finish with some quiet time; you can meditate, lie down, or visualize something that makes you feel good. The main objective is to feel the energy that you have just reclaimed!

Think about it; you can now use this new, free energy to focus on what you want and manifest it into your dream reality!

Finally, visualize yourself being cloaked in a luminescent blanket of energetic protection. Feel the blanket all over your body.

This is your new energetic boundary!

Set an intention that this boundary remains in place as you step confidently forward into your day.

The next step is to re-write your beliefs. Awareness is everything!

I see so many people who get stuck in releasing old energies and negative beliefs or programs. Yet, instead of quickly replacing those old beliefs with some new, more empowering beliefs, they just spend all their time resenting their old selves.

The Universe likes to move fast. You need to practice releasing what no longer serves you while quickly replacing it with something new.
It's like getting rid of your old clothes. You also need to get some new ones, right? Unless you want to walk around naked, resenting some old-fashioned clothes, you are still "trying to get rid of."

After creating new beliefs, align your actions with them.

For example: *If now I choose to believe that money is safe and not evil, maybe I can scale my business?*

Finally, learning how Facebook ads work is fun and exciting. I no longer feel bad about expanding myself and my work.

The Love of Attraction

I used to believe that putting myself out there with my work wasn't safe. But now, I have a new belief. I know that sharing my work is my purpose; it's who I am. And so, it's normal for me to take massive aligned action and follow my passion.

Or:

If I choose to believe that love is safe, and I can be loved for who I am, I no longer need to pretend I'm someone else. Now, I can just be myself and easily attract the man or woman of my dreams.

Secret #7 Release This Invisible Manifestation Killer

Do you have an invisible ceiling that makes you sabotage your actions?

For example, you think you're worthy and deserving of making a certain amount of money. You have a safe zone. But, you can't even think about expanding it.

Or, perhaps, you think love has a limit. Maybe you attracted a great partner, and things are marvelous, but you start thinking thoughts such as: *OK, it can't be that good, come on. I'm sure eventually he or she will stop treating me that well.*

And so, your fear-based mindsets create a reality of fear.
Fear is fueled by contraction. In contrast, love is driven by expansion.

Think just like the Universe does. Don't be afraid to think big!

So many people choose to focus on the negative and get addicted to it. Example:
-Now, it can only get worse
-When you start making money, it will not last forever

The Love of Attraction

-The more you are in a relationship, the less love you feel for each other!

Why choose to focus on going down if you can keep going up? The way you talk to yourself and others is essential. Stop expecting things to get worse and mindfully choose to expect them to get better.

Looking up and expanding your horizons doesn't mean you're not feeling grateful for what you have now. Yes, continue your gratitude for everything you have now.

But, at the same time, let the Universe know that you are open to receiving new levels of love, success, health, and happiness.

The Universe doesn't know any limits. So, choose to think as the Universe does, and stop feeling guilty for choosing to expand your horizons.

You like your job? Good! Because now, every day you love it more and more! You eat healthily and exercise? Great! Now, every day it's more and more fun. Are you in love? Fantastic! Now, every day, you get to experience more and more of it.

Choosing to stick to your invisible limitations is like closing yourself in a basement. Why not expand instead?

Secret #8 The Liberating Essence of Letting Go

Most people try to let go, and they actually resist what they try to let go of. All their identity is focused on the act of letting go and releasing.

The real secret lies in understanding your emotions. We can't just sit still. We always rush, looking for the next thing to do. And so, we don't experience the present moment.

Every single feeling you have brings up different thoughts. The source is always the same, though- your core feeling or feelings.

For example, let's say you want to start a new business, and you get a thought: *oh, but what if I fail?*

That thought comes from the feeling of fear and anxiety (because of some past event).

Thoughts are just thoughts. But we all attached a feeling to it, based on our internal data, such as things that went wrong in the past, what we're not good at, or because someone else failed to do what we want to do.

Most of our suffering arises because we identify with our ego.

The Love of Attraction

Emotion consists of a thought and feelings attached to it (based on past events). The unity of heart and mind creates our reality. But it's up to us to choose love instead of fear.

Something happens, we express what's happening, we become a part of that feeling, but the rest of it goes to our unconsciousness.

Any event is simply a trigger. The event in itself doesn't necessarily make you emotional.

For example, two people can get stuck in traffic. One can feel happy listening to their favorite songs and just intending to unwind or get in a good mood. But, other person chooses to complain, get angry, and indulge in low vibrations. Perhaps getting stuck in traffic makes them feel hopeless or triggers some traumatic experience. No judgment here.

When our feelings are too strong, we want to get unconscious by using food, TV, tobacco, scrolling on social media, being rude to other people, etc. We want to escape what's there, and we divert our attention outwards to not deal with anything.

We love suppressing and holding our feelings down. Escapism and suppression go hand in hand. Instead of feeling fear and surrendering it, we express it and replay it over and over again.

We also love repressing, which is unconscious. This is when old emotions get deep into the unconscious and keep boiling up until something triggers them.

Physical pain, insomnia, anxiety usually come because of repressed feelings. So, how to indeed release and be free from old fears haunting us?

Let's say you feel fearful.

You acknowledge the feeling first without any labels and resistance. You give yourself permission to fully feel it. There will be resistance, and you might feel a bit guilty for not suppressing it. Say: *I allow myself to handle this, with love, all from a place of love.*
Embrace that feeling fully. Finally, ask yourself: *Am I willing to let go and stop holding onto this feeling of fear, this grudge, this past experience?*

Even if you know the answer, please ask yourself several times: *am I really ready to let go?*

Real letting go is hard because we built our identities around it. Like I already mentioned, some people never let go. They are always stuck *trying* to let go. They are so used to hold on to their identity, and now, they try to let go without fully stepping into the new chapter of their lives. They still stick to an identity built around some old events or traumas. It's just now they do it from what they think is a better place (because they logically understand the concept of letting go).

When you finally let go, looking back at your past seems like looking at some past life or a different person.

Being triggered can be a good thing because now you know what you need to work on (as we said, such a trigger is just the feedback from the Universe).

There's nothing wrong with expressing how you feel or indulging in activities that make you feel good. But use them mindfully. Perhaps you like to watch a funny movie to laugh and have a good time, or you enjoy a glass of wine over a nice dinner with friends. However, you don't use these activities to escape your feelings.

Also, don't get stuck with labeling your judgments. And don't fear the fact that you're feeling fear. Instead, be mindfully grateful that now you have an awareness of the power of love.

Secret #9 Your Healthy, Love-Based Boundaries

To attract what you want, you need to mindfully protect yourself from what is holding you back. Luckily, there are many energy and mindset tools you can use. You can use love as your magic shield!

So why do you need personal boundaries? Well, look at anyone who has established success and wealth. All those people set healthy boundaries in their businesses, health, and personal life. Healthy boundaries are essential.

It's a skill you acquire as you grow. Sometimes you need to use masculine energy and force your new boundaries. If you are like me, an empath, you love helping people and giving, you may find it hard.

For example, I used to be always available on social media. I felt guilty if I couldn't reply to someone as soon as I saw their message. I thought I was on a mission to help everyone with everything. I totally ignored the fact that some people just wanted to pick my brains with no intention to ever purchase anything from me. Some didn't even intend to use my free information to improve their lives. They just wanted to chat or meet some people online. I felt terrible for not replying, and so I kept replying. Such a vicious cycle because I was always busy but not productive. Because of that, I neglected the most crucial activities (such as writing new books) to really help me grow.

I didn't have any energy left to write. I felt drained because of many energy vampires who wanted to take advantage of me. Of course, now, I don't blame them. I blame the fact that back then, I didn't have any healthy boundaries.

So, I had to learn it the hard way. I also realized that people on the other side didn't really understand that writing and publishing was something important to me. They thought I was doing it as a hobby. It's all because I didn't set boundaries and didn't consciously position myself and my brand.

I was acting out of fear: *"Oh, what will they think of me?"*. But, finally, I had to switch to loved-based boundaries. I had to create my schedule and stick to it. My main focus is writing, and I write for a particular reader avatar- curious and ambitious souls. These people appreciate my work and value my time (because they want me to write more!)

Then, after the most crucial writing and other publishing activities are accomplished, I check my email. There's no more stress or fear. I feel happy and balanced.

Now, all areas of life are interconnected. You need to understand your limitations. Suppose you always give up your boundaries in business/work. In that case, you may also get seduced by different temptations in health, such as indulging in fast food instead of cooking a healthy, wholesome meal.

For example, when I lacked boundaries in my professional life, I couldn't stick to a healthy lifestyle. Instead, I would get tempted to order pizza or some fast food.

So, ask yourself what makes you feel stressed and uncomfortable? Give yourself some time of honesty and think about what is right for you. Yes, I know for many of you it may seem a bit ego-based. But the truth is, if you want to help others, you need to help yourself first.

If you want freedom, you need a system. And you can't create a system when you lack boundaries and live in chaos.

People may leave you or your space when you set boundaries—no judgment, nothing wrong with them or you. By setting boundaries, you make it clear what your vibration is.

You can be the nicest person on this planet but still, have your boundaries. Anyone or anything that stresses you is unacceptable. Apply this rule across different areas of your life.

Tune into your feelings. In your gut, you know when something is wrong. Yes, you can excuse other people and keep justifying other people while slowly and surely start resenting them. You ignore your feelings, and eventually, resentment (which is very low vibration) is created.

Recognize your feelings early on. If you feel resentment towards yourself or other people, it means you didn't set your boundaries. Yes, allow yourself to feel annoyed. It's good that those feelings are coming out! Remember, it's just feedback. Ignoring your feelings means you are neglecting your existence. Act upon your feelings!

Discomfort and resentment (if it's more severe) indicate a lack of boundaries. Use it as feedback from the Universe and your higher self and do something about it.

What is your inner discomfort level? Give yourself an honest score (from one to ten). If you gave yourself seven or more, ask yourself what exactly is bothering you.

For example, you run a business, you hire people. You want to be a cool boss and allow your employees to be creative. You don't want to micromanage your team; you want to trust them. But then, a few months pass, and you realize you're not getting the results you wanted. You start feeling like a fool because your employees are taking advantage of you and your goodwill.

The real problem, though, is your lack of boundaries. As a person with healthy boundaries, you can communicate your vision and expectations and what is and isn't allowed—all in a kind, loved-based but firm way.

Switching to a loved-based mindset doesn't mean you must always agree with everyone. This can be a fear-based mindset. You feel scared to share how you really feel. So, keep your healthy boundaries and communicate them to others kindly.

The first step is forgiveness. It's all about learning. So, don't feel bad! Address your emotions first. Remember? Feelings are just feedback. Now you can mindfully change your reactions.

The second step is your communication. Be clear and specific and let other people know what they can and can't expect. People can't read your mind (unless they have some superpowers!)

Don't be afraid to protect yourself from negative energies. For example, I used to share too much about my business and private life, even with people I didn't know very well. I would just go on and on and explain everything that was going on, all with good intention. But then, I realized that some people would either get jealous or gossip. So, I had to learn to keep certain things to myself. I had to understand who I could confide in. Now, when someone I don't really know that well asks me about some specific business stuff or numbers, I politely say: *"Well, I only share this information with my accountant and the tax office, of course."* And we both start laughing!

When someone I hardly know asks me about my personal life, I like to answer with humor: *"Oh, it's OK, but probably wouldn't make a good soap opera."*

As a self-employed person working from home, I also had to set my work and life balance boundaries. Firstly, I had to set them with myself. I know this may seem weird to so many people who just get up and drive to their workplace.

But I also know that those working from home may sometimes struggle with their schedule and boundaries. And now, with the post lockdown reality, more and more people are forced to work from home.

So, once again, I had to use my masculine energy to develop a specific schedule. Wake up at a particular time, get the most important writing and business stuff done early in the morning.

Then, I had to communicate my boundaries and schedule to my family. I explained to them that working for myself doesn't mean I'm always free and available and that if I don't stick to my schedule, I won't be successful.

I also got two different phone numbers, one for work, another for my family. So, now, when I switch from work, I'm available for my family. Since I'm more productive during the week and follow my schedule, I can enjoy life-work balance and unwind on weekends and be fully present for my family and friends, instead of worrying I have so much to do.

Keep auditing yourself. This work never ends. Keep observing your behaviors and boundaries, as well as the way you communicate them to others.

You may realize that you're affected by the way you were raised and your family's role. For example: *to be a good daughter, I have to behave in a certain way.*

Perhaps some family members can always influence or convince you to do something because they know your weaknesses?

Be aware that some people may be taking advantage of you (doesn't mean they are bad people, but they just got used to specific patterns). Are you in *give and take* relationships, or is it *only give give give*?

Also, be mindful and respect other people's boundaries and preferences.

I recently found myself feeling lots of resentment towards my younger sister. It got triggered during a conversation we had about business. I was very excited to share a new idea I got after reading one of my favorite love-based marketing authors. And my sister said something like: *"Don't even compare yourself to this author. She is on a much higher level. You're not really that successful. So, I'm not too sure this could work for you."*

At first, it really hurt me. I had a good intention and just wanted to share some ideas that I knew could help my sister. I wasn't comparing myself to anyone. What really triggered me is the fact that I always shared everything I learned with my sister. She's now pretty successful in her business because of one idea I shared with her a few years ago while giving her the exact steps to follow. So, feeling a bit sad, I thought to myself: "I helped her so much, and now, instead of gratitude, I'm getting some mixed messages!"
But then, after diving more in-depth, I realized a few things:
-my sister was in lots of stress because her health wasn't very good; she was on medication and in lots of pain. And I chose to talk about business, which probably made her a bit tired. She was on holiday and wanted to unwind. She even told me she didn't want to talk about work or business, but I just kept talking.
-when we were kids, our parents would always compare her to me ("you should learn from Elena, she was always good at

geography," "why did you get a C minus? Elena was always an A or B student, maybe she can help you with your exam?")

And yes, our parents had good intentions too. But once again, childhood and adulthood are two different journeys.

One needs to learn to let go. Some patterns and behaviors might have been helpful to us at some point when we were kids. But now, they can irritate us and cause us discomfort.

When setting and respecting boundaries for ourselves, we must also respect other people's boundaries. In my case, I didn't respect my sister's wishes and boundaries. I kept talking about topics she didn't want to talk about, therefore triggering a somehow ironic response.

It all ended up well. We're all right now. But we had to have an honest family conversation to ensure everyone was OK and everyone was treating everyone else well. No irony and no passive-aggressive remarks!

To sum up this story, you should never tolerate any negative remarks you get from your family and friends.

But also ask yourself what triggered them. Did you respect their boundaries? Were you empathic? Do you actually understand where they're coming from?

Healthy boundaries also prevent burnout. Now, to clarify where I stand on taking action - if you've read any of my previous books, you know I'm all about taking action. I don't believe in just sitting around, mindlessly repeating your wishes and waiting for them to magically materialize. I'm all for taking mindful, aligned action to show the Universe that you're committed.

But at the same time, I'm not for *hustle hustle hustle* mentality. Yes, it may work for some people, which is excellent. Everyone is different.
This is where your personal boundaries come up. You need to decide what works for you long-term. For example, if I took action based entirely on what other people do, I'd burn out.

I used to stress out about pushing harder and tried to sleep less to get more done. I followed young people who could easily do with five or six hours of sleep. But my body rebelled.

I knew I needed more rest. So, I no longer feel guilty about sleeping more. I know I need eight to nine hours of sleep, and some time to fall asleep, meditate and unwind. I like to wake up feeling well-rested.

In other words, I honor my self-care and my feelings. And I base my self-care on what I need to do, not on what others are doing.

And not on the latest trend (as for what we must eat, do, and how to sleep).

Now I'm in a better place, and I can be a better friend, family member, and entrepreneur. I no longer feel guilty about setting up some *me* time.

Ask yourself, how often do you replenish your energy with loved-based boundaries so that you can experience love-based vibrations and manifest faster?

Secret #10 When Making Mistakes is Important If You Want to Attract Abundance

Many people say if you keep repeating failure, it's probably a negative pattern. And yes, it's definitely true.

We already know that negative situations and patterns are feedback.

But at the same time, if you've read any biography of successful people, you will quickly realize that they failed a lot!

They see failures as a lesson, not a mistake. From an energetic level, it's interesting to look at negative patterns around each so-called "failure" and do some energy work with a healer to remove trapped negative energy. I'm all for energy work!

But from a pure mindset level, in our case, love-based mindset...

It's all about learning! Looking back on my journey as an entrepreneur, I regret that I didn't fail more. Because I know that all the success and abundance I could attract was because I could learn from my mistakes.

I could write an entire book talking about projects I tried and failed with. But looking back, all those past experiences made me wiser and stronger. They helped me change my brain so that now I can make better decisions.

I've failed in different ventures (as self-employed) and various jobs I tried for various companies in multiple sectors.

For a long time, I felt very ashamed because I couldn't stick to one path successfully. And yes, I did lots of energy work desperately trying to get rid of negative energy. Nothing wrong with energy work.

But the best energy work is when you combine it with mindset work (and vice versa). Energy work is working with your heart; mindset work is more about working with your head. In this physical world, we need both.

So, I gave myself permission to make mistakes! I decided to own the fact that I had the privilege to work in different sectors. I felt grateful I tried different jobs and businesses and learned a lot as a result.

Are you an ambitious soul who dreams about attracting incredible abundance? Do you want to build an internationally recognized company? Perhaps you want to become a famous author, artist, or self-employed professional. Well, whatever your dreams are, you need to be OK with making mistakes. Use them to learn as much as you can.

The same rule applies to other areas of your life. Perhaps you desire to attract a loving partner. Yet, you got stuck in a vicious cycle of attracting people you find negative. Well, at least now you know what you don't like, and so, you can set an intention to attract precisely the opposite, in a healthy, love-based way.

You want vibrant health. In alignment with that, you try different diets. Yet they all fail! Well, at least now, you know what not to do. And so, you can simplify your wellness quest by creating your own diet!

Perhaps you want to follow your passion and become a blogger. You put in lots of work learning how the online world works. You keep creating valuable content. Yet you can't grow your following because you realize you didn't choose the right niche and feel stuck. Well, at least now, you know how blogging works. You can now set a new blog in a new category and do it much better!

Remember, you don't fail, you succeed or you learn. So, be passionate about learning. As you stay open to learning, you also open yourself to receiving new signs from the Universe! Everything is unfolding as it should! Eliminate the word "failure" from your vocabulary. Instead, be curious about learning and growing.

Personal Message from Elena

Thank You so much for reading this book to the very end! I hope you found it inspiring and discovered at least one helpful idea to help you grow on your Law of Attraction journey.

If you have a few minutes, I'd really appreciate it if you could leave me a short review on Amazon. Let other LOA readers in our community know who this book can help and why.
Thank You Thank You Thank You,
I hope we "meet" again,
Much love,

Elena

For more information and resources about LOA, please visit my website:

www.LOAforSuccess.com

If you'd like to say hi, please email me at
elena@LOAforSuccess.com

Free LOA Newsletter + Bonus Gift

To help you AMPLIFY what you've learned in this book, I'd like to offer you a free copy of my **LOA Workbook – a powerful, FREE 5-day program (eBook & audio)** designed to help you raise your vibration while eliminating resistance and negativity.

To sign up for free, visit the link below now:

www.loaforsuccess.com/newsletter

You'll also get free access to my highly acclaimed, uplifting **LOA Newsletter.**

Through this email newsletter, I regularly share all you need to know about the manifestation mindset and energy.

My newsletter alone helped hundreds of my readers manifest their own desires.

Plus, whenever I release a new book, you can get it at a deeply discounted price or even for free.

You can also start receiving my new audiobooks published on Audible at no cost!

To sign up for free, visit the link below now:

www.loaforsuccess.com/newsletter

I'd love to connect with you and stay in touch with you while helping you on your LOA journey!

If you happen to have any technical issues with your sign up, please email us at:

support@LOAforSuccess.com

More Books by Elena G. Rivers

Money Mindset: Stop Manifesting What You Don't Want and Shift Your Subconscious Mind into Money & Abundance

How Not to Manifest: Manifestation Mistakes to Avoid and How to Finally Make LOA Work for You

Visualization Demystified: The Untold Secrets to Re-Program Your Subconscious Mind and Manifest Your Dream Reality in 5 Simple Steps

Law of Attr-Action for Entrepreneurs: Advanced Identity Shifting Secrets to Manifest the Income & Impact You Deserve

Law of Attraction & Manifestation: 6 in 1 Edition

More books available at:

www.LOAforSuccess.com

www.ingramcontent.com/pod-product-compliance
Lightning Source LLC
Chambersburg PA
CBHW071812080526
44589CB00012B/769